Examining Doctrines
Vision for the 21st Century and Beyond!

By Donald A. Peart

Examining Doctrines©2012 Donald A. Peart

All rights are reserved. However, this book may be reproduced for inclusion of brief quotations in review.

ISBN: 978-0-9886897-0-1

Cover design by Jeshua Peart

Dedication

The book is dedicated to all who are willing to "hear" the words contained herein.

Acknowledgments

I honor the Spirit of Jesus, "for it seemed good to the Holy Spirit;" "the Spirit of wisdom and revelation," to inspire me to write this book.[1] I also gladly acknowledge all my teachers who have taught me many things through the years.

In addition, honor my beautiful wife, Judith (who is beautiful both internally and externally) for her partnership with me in Jesus' priest-work. To my children (Donald Jr. and his wife Keyanna, Jeshua, Charity, Benjamin, and Jesse), may the doctrine of Christ remain in you, into the age.

---

[1] Acts 15:28a; Ephesians 1:17; Galatians 2:2

Honors

Due to the topic of this book, it seems appropriate to honor the apostles' doctrines of the New Testament: The apostle's doctrines of God as first taught by "the apostle and High Priest of our 'confession,' Jesus Christ;"[2] the "doctrine of Christ,"[3] as taught by the original twelve apostles of the Lamb; and the gospel of Jesus Christ, as received and taught by the apostles of the Spirit through the revelation of the Holy Spirit. [4] I also honor the prophets of the Old and New Testaments who prophesied of the sufferings of Christ and those who represents Christ by the Spirit of Christ who was in them.[5] I also honor the apostles and prophets of this age who have continued to pioneer in the Spirit of Jesus to restore the doctrine of Christ.

---

[2] Hebrews 3:1
[3] 2 John 1:7-11
[4] Ephesians 3:3-5
[5] 1 Peter 1:10-12; Ephesians 3:5

Table of Contents

Examining Doctrines 5
Winds of Doctrines 9
How to Know the Doctrines From God 21
Jesus' Doctrine of Vision 26
Doctrine of Purpose 33
Doctrine of Duality 39
The Doctrine of SelfAppointments 43
The Doctrine of the "Rapture" 48
The Doctrine of Giving 71
Reviewing Doctrines 81

Examining Doctrines

Galatians 2:1-2: ¹*Then fourteen years after I went up again to Jerusalem with Barnabas, and took Titus with [me] also. ²And I went up by revelation, and **communicated unto them that gospel which I preach** among the Gentiles, but **privately** to them which were of reputation, lest by any means I should run, or had run, in vain.*

Doctrines of men (mine or others') should be able to be examined for "exactness,"⁶ as the Lord may require. The 21st Century should be a century of "exact" teaching, not just accurate teaching. Doctrines were examined on a regular basis by the apostles in the days of the original twelve apostles of the lamb and the apostles of the Spirit, like Paul, Barnabas, Silas, Timothy, and so on. Apostles **did** "confer" or hold "conferences" with each other with respect to doctrinal issues. Yet, I must also say that God may not direct some apostles and prophets to **"immediately confer** with flesh and blood," as we see in the example of Paul (Galatians 1:16).

However, Paul was such a transparent apostle that he submitted his doctrine to the apostolic pillars (Peter, James, and John) at Jerusalem; and he also confronted publicly apostles who were walking contrary to "straight-footed" doctrine (Galatians 2). Paul submitting his doctrine for examination was **"by revelation."**

This may explain why some of the current administrators of the gospel of Jesus are so reluctant to have their doctrines examined. Maybe, they have no revelation from the Lord Jesus, thus they may be afraid of exposure that they have no "Rock" for a

---

⁶ Refer to Acts 18:26, where the phrase "more perfectly" is translated from the Greek word "akribesteron" which literally means "exact."

foundation. It appears that they need **a revelation** from the Lord that "conferences" were originally intended to discuss doctrine by dialog, and not by, or for dogmatic assertions.

In Acts 15, the elders came together to examine the doctrine of circumcision in the flesh, and determined by dialog with each other and dialog with the Holy Spirit that the doctrine of circumcision in the flesh did not apply to the Gentile Christians. Thus, as was stated in Acts 2:42, it was the "apostles' doctrine" that the newly birthed Church "continued in.". The same should be true today; the doctrine[7] of true apostles and prophets should be **"consulted"**[8] by the Church.

As indicated earlier, in the New Testament, "conferences" were held for the leaders, and not necessarily for the saints (Galatians 2:1; 2:6). Conferences in the early Church were not held for money or for gathering of the saints to see who can gather the largest crowd. On the contrary, conferences were usually for the apostles and prophets to discuss doctrinal issues, to resolve the issues through the answers ascertained together-with the Holy Spirit, then the apostles and prophets distribute the doctrine of the Lord to the saints. (Galatians 2, Acts 15, Acts 15:22, 27, 32).

Today, it appears that some ministers of the gospel are not as willing as the apostle Paul to hold conferences that may or may not "add" to the doctrine they are already preaching (Galatians 2). It also appears in today's doctrinal cultures that if conflicts arise over doctrines, the Holy Spirit is also not consulted corporately as He was consulted by the apostles and elders in

---

[7] Note: "the apostles' doctrine" should be "the doctrine of Christ," a Christ-centered doctrine and not a man-centered doctrine; the prophets' doctrine should also be Jesus-centered and not worldly.

[8] Another definition for the Greek word translated in the King James as "conferred" and "conference" in Galatians 1:16; 2:16 respectively.

Acts 15:6; 28. Ministers of the 21st Century have to follow the pattern of the first leaders of the Church.

In the 21st Century, the apostles and elders must receive the "revelation" to "confer" with each other by the impression of the Holy Spirit. One of the purposes of conferring with one another is to remove the traditions and doctrines of men that make God's word of non-effect (compare Mark 7:13; Matthew 15:7-9). Paul went to Jerusalem "by revelation" to "communicate" his doctrine to the other apostles (Galatians 2:2). We learn from Paul's example that conferences are to be held by revelation of the Holy Spirit as it was in the days of the first apostles. Conferences are to be held to discuss doctrines to verify that we are not "running in vain."

Paul, Peter, James, and John gave us the pattern of conferences as a venue to clarify doctrines (Galatians 2). However, manmade doctrines have turned conferences into a money-making business. **Let us be different in the 21st Century and beyond.** Let us abide in the apostles' doctrines as outlined in the New Testament. Let us "by revelation" submit our doctrine to peer review like Paul did in Galatians 2:1-9; and if there are conflicts with respect to doctrines, let us meet to resolve doctrinal issues as they did in Acts 15:1-35!

> *¹Then fourteen years after I went up again to Jerusalem with Barnabas, and took Titus with me also. ²And I went up **by revelation**, and **communicated unto them that gospel which I preach** among the Gentiles, but privately to them which were of reputation, least by any means I should run, or had run, in vain ... ⁶But of these who seemed to be somewhat, (whatsoever they were, it makes no matter to me: God accepts no man's person:) for they who seemed to be somewhat in **conference added** nothing to me **(Galatians 2:1-6).***

> ¹*And certain men which came down from Judaea taught the brethren, and said, except you be circumcised after the manner of Moses, you cannot be saved. ²When therefore Paul and Barnabas had no small dissension and disputation with them, they determined that Paul and Barnabas, and certain other of them, should go up to Jerusalem unto the apostles and elders about this question ... ⁶And **the apostles and elders came together for to consider** of this matter (Acts 15:1-6).*

Thus, this book is part one of a series of books to be set forth in an attempt to discuss and/or clarify some of the controversial doctrines of our day. Coupled with this book, a series of conferences will be held by our ministry starting in 2012 and beyond. I encourage you to "abide in the doctrine of Christ!" That is, preach doctrine that emphasizes everything about Jesus and His finished work.

> ⁹*Whoever transgresses and does not abide in **the doctrine of Christ** does not have God. He who **abides** in the doctrine of Christ has both the Father and the Son.   ¹⁰If anyone comes to you and does not bring this doctrine, do not receive him into your house nor greet him; ¹¹for he who greets him shares in his evil deeds (**2 John 1:9-11**).*

Winds of Doctrines

Ephesians 4:14: *That we [henceforth] be no more children, tossed to and fro, and carried about with every **wind of doctrine**, by the sleight of men, [and] cunning craftiness, whereby they lie in wait to deceive.*

Paul declared in the reference above that "doctrine" is considered as "wind." In this generation, "winds of doctrines" are blowing some saints all over the place. It seems like every minister has his or her "own" doctrine and not the doctrine that comes from God. Some in this generation are like the Corinthian Church; "everyone has a psalm, everyone has a doctrine, everyone has a tongue, everyone has a revelation, everyone has an interpretation" (see 1 Corinthians 14:26). So, how do we know the doctrines from God with so many voices in the earth? This will be discussed later.

In addition, Jesus prophesied of **windy days**, through His angel, to the apostle John, in the book of Revelation, that the "winds" would blow on the earth. Jesus also spoke of the **"winds"** that test the strength of the house founded upon the Rock, versus the house that was founded upon sand (Matthew 7:24-28). In this age, some are still experiencing the "every wind of doctrine" that Paul discussed and that the apostle John signified in Revelation 6:12 through Revelation 7:1-3. However, God has angels that will control the wind until His bond-slaves are sealed with the Holy Spirit.[9]

Paul declared "that we should no longer be children, tossed to and fro and carried about with every wind of doctrine"

---

[9] Revelation 7:1-3; Ephesians 1:13

(Ephesians 4:14). In the sixth seal, John saw a "mega wind"[10] that caused the stars of heaven to fall due to immaturity[11] (Revelation 6). In Revelation 7, the "wind" was so harmful to the earth that it had to be stopped until the servants of God were sealed in their foreheads. Thus, winds of doctrines are a serious matter. With that said, let us now look at the apostle Paul, and the apostle John; and for additional reference, we will also look at the writings of Jeremiah the prophet relative to the various winds of doctrine that can affect the immature.

> *[11]And He Himself gave some to be apostles, some prophets, some evangelists, and some pastors and teachers, [12]for the equipping of the saints for the work of ministry, for the edifying of the body of Christ, [13]till we all come to the unity of the faith and of the knowledge of the Son of God, to a perfect man, to the measure of the stature of the fullness of Christ; [14]that we should no longer be **children, tossed to and fro** and carried about with **every wind of doctrine**, by the **trickery of men**, in the cunning craftiness of deceitful plotting* **(Ephesians 4:11-14).**

Paul indicated that "children" can be "'billowed (dashed over) by the sea' and 'carried-all-about' with **every wind of doctrine."** Thus, immaturity, symbolized by "children," can cause immature persons to be blown about by every wind of doctrine. Briefly speaking, maturity in Christ is attaining to the same faith (oneness with His faith) that Jesus attained as the Son of God, and attaining the same knowledge that Jesus acquired as the Son of God (Ephesians 4:13). This will be discussed a little further in the chapter that discusses the doctrine of vision. With that said,

---

[10] The wind that is mentioned in the 6th Seal (Revelation 6) and in Revelation 7 seems to have reference to natural wind and spiritual winds (doctrines).
[11] This "fall due to immaturity" will be explained later.

here are four (4) of signs that every wind of doctrine is affecting a person.

1. The effect of "every wind of doctrine" is like "children being tossed to and fro" which literally means, like a "non-speaking child," a person can be easily pushed around by windy doctrines like the wind can cause "a surge of the sea."

2. The effect of "every wind of doctrine" is also like a child being carried-all-about" by a strong wind that is overwhelming to the child.

3. The effect of "every wind of doctrine" is also like "children ... carried about" by "dice playing," or "gambling," or "slyness," of men "in all-working."

4. The effect of "every wind of doctrine" is also like "children ... carried about" "in change-road of seduction"

As can be seen above "every wind of doctrine" is compared to "a surge of the sea," among other things. That is, doctrine has the potential overwhelm the non-speaking Christians like a surging sea. Winds of doctrines are also likened to being influenced by dice playing and gambling of men. That is, men who exercise their nonsense in winds of doctrines "gamble" in choosing messages they deliver. Jesus said, that some "cannot hear God," therefore, some gamble with their Sunday sermons. So, with that said, let us look at the influence of the "sea" first.

What are some of the symbolic meaning of "sea?" The Scripture compares the "troubled ("divorced") sea" to the wicked (Isaiah 57:20). The "great sea" and "many waters" also symbolizes "peoples, multitudes, nations and tongues" (Revelation 17:1,

17:15; Daniel 7, Revelation 13:1). The sea ("water") is also a symbol of humanity that is sexually unstable (Genesis 49:3-4). Thus, the sea symbolizes the sea of humanity who is in affect divorced from God. It follows that the winds of doctrine are taught by those who are influenced by the surge of the sea of humanity, rather than being influenced by "the will of God;" and those who are indeed carried about by the waves of unstable humanity are indeed children themselves. Thus, we can tell children who are tosses by the sea surge of doctrines, they become wet with the same doctrine and may imbibe the sea water.

Saying it another way, doctrines which are spotted by the world's teachings (the world being symbolized by the "sea of humanity") are considered "wind of doctrine" that cause the immature to divorce God and His Church and to wander from God. The doctrine of the Church of Jesus should not imitate the doctrine of the world (the sea of humanity). We learned earlier, in Isaiah, the troubled or divorced sea is compared to the wicked. In the book of Daniel 7 and Revelation 13, the beast comes from the "'vast' sea." In the book of Revelation 12:12, we can learn that there are basically three realms, the heavens dwellers, the earth dwellers, and the sea dwellers.

Those who are sea dwellers, the false-teachers, false-prophets, false-apostles, and false-shepherds are constantly affected by the surges of the sea of humanity, and they teach doctrines that cause instability in immature saints. Here are some practical examples of doctrines that are influenced by the surge of the sea of humanity:

> 1. Some preachers teach more of what they learn from movies, the news, secular shows, celebrities, fables, and

seminary, rather than what the living Word of God and the living Holy Spirit teaches.

2. The world's doctrine of "divorce" is more prevalent in the Church rather than the doctrine of God concerning covenant marriage.

How can a person claim to manage God's Church and yet he/she cannot maintain a marriage without divorce or multiple divorces? One of the qualifications to be an elder[12] is that a man is supposed to be the husband of the "first wife." He is not to be a husband of one wife at a time, or multiple wives. Yet, according to Ezekiel 47, there will be grace for some of the divorced.

The other point that Paul brought out relative to every wind of doctrine is that wind of doctrine causes "children to be carried about," here and there with "trickery." "Trickery" is the Greek word "cube," which literally means "dicey," dice playing, gambling, sly, and so on. This sounds like some of the practices of today. Some so-called men of God do more guessing of what message to speak, rather than spending the time with "the Great-Togetherness" and giving the effort it takes to hear God's "Rhema" — words from a living person. Instead, unprepared "instructors" roll the dice; and the dice say, this message today; maybe this message tomorrow, with no "hearing" from the Spirit of God (contrast Isaiah 26:9).

---

[12] The phrase "elder" (masculine (presbyteros) is also used of "elder women" in 1 Timothy 5:2. That is, women can be called "elders." Hence, a "aged women" (presbytis, feminine of presbyteros) should strive to be the wife of her first husband. Yet, there is room for mercy! Compare Jesus' dealings with the woman that had five husbands in John 4; and Jesus' principle on why divorce usually occurs in Matthew 19:8.

People are all over the place following "the gambling of men." Some gamble their souls with this prophet today, another prophet tomorrow and yet again gamble that they will get "a word" from a different prophet the next day. Or today, this apostle is "the one;" tomorrow another apostle is "the one." Further, people change ministers like some ministers change spouses nowadays. As indicated earlier, one of the qualifications to be an elder is that a man is supposed to be the husband of his "first wife."

Yet, the Church should have a plurality of ministers, and not one man centered. So, I am not teaching exclusivism with regards to certain ministers. The pattern is many elders over one Church, not one elder (bishop) over many Churches (Acts 20:17; 28; 1 Peter 5:1-4). The Church should not be hindered from fellowshipping with one another ((3 John 1:9). We are also no longer in a "one-man" show in the Churches (the big "I" (apostles, prophets, pastors, etc.) and the little "you" (those who are not apostles, prophets, or pastors)). Conversely, we are not supposed to be "carried about" after every one who calls himself a prophet, or apostle, or evangelist who has "dicey" doctrines (1 John 4:1).

Some pseudo ministers determine their wind of doctrine according to the count of the dice that they roll (guess). That is, they guess at what to preach, rather than hearing from God (Romans 10:14-16). They also follow signs rather than God's "today voice." Jesus calls those who seek for signs a wicked and adulterous generation (Matthew 12:38-39).

Their dice may roll a six (the number of man) today, so they teach a man-centered gospel instead of a Christ centered doctrine (2 Corinthians 4:5). Their dice may roll the number one (1) another day, and they teach about some erroneous sign about the unification of the various denominations which has nothing to do with the real meaning of Ephesians 4:13.

With that said, the sixth seal, as opened by the Lamb of God (Jesus), also discussed the perils of the wind that can be applied to the perils of the doctrines of men. In the 6th Seal, the wind (of doctrine) causes the stars of heaven to fall or sway like immature figs (Revelation 6:13). The stars can be symbolic of children and the wind symbolic of doctrine. With respect to "wind" (of doctrine) that can cause an immature person to sway, I am reminded of an event that occurred when I was invited to a Church to preach.

The pastor of the house I preached in was very religious (full of outward show of piety); and it was apparent that he did not have a relationship with the Lord. In the Spirit, I also kept sensing (seeing) something strange around his loins. (It was later revealed that this pastor was having sexual relations with the parishioners, and the Lord closed that Church about 30 days after the encounter with him).

During the meeting, this pastor attempted to sway the Church, including some of the saints who came with me, with what I call "vain (empty) worship." He kept attempting inciting them in the flesh to participate in what was obviously "unsuccessful" worship. In fact, it could be likened to the antic of the prophets of Baal that Elijah exposed as fraudulent. It seemed to me he was attempting to kindle his own fire (Isaiah 50:11). As this occurred, I literally saw in the Spirit the saints who came with me being blown upon sideways by a wind to sway them. They were indeed blown upon; however, they were not moved by that wind because they held the doctrine of Jesus Christ in them. It is also worthy to note that this pastor did not believe our hearing and declaration as heard and declared by Isaiah concerning

Jesus' ugliness (Romans 10:16; Isaiah 53:1-2). In other words, it appears that God may have removed this candlestick, as I indicated above, because the pastor denied Jesus' ugliness (part of the doctrine of Christ) and redemption. With that said, the sixth seal does indeed reveal that there will be an era when some will fall by a "mega wind" — a mega wind of doctrine. Let us compare some scriptures.

> *That we should no longer be children, tossed to and fro and carried about with every **wind of doctrine**, by the trickery of men, in the cunning craftiness of deceitful plotting **(Ephesians 4:14).***

> *[12] I looked when He opened the sixth seal, and behold, there was a great earthquake; and the sun became black as sackcloth of hair, and the moon became like blood. [13] And the **stars of heaven fell** to the earth, as a fig tree drops its late figs when it is shaken by a **mighty wind (Revelation 6:12-13)***

When the sixth Seal was opened, one of the events that occurred as a result is that a "mega wind" caused the stars of heaven to fall like late or unripe figs. We have learned from the apostle Paul that "wind" is also a symbol of "doctrine." In Genesis we also learn that the sun is a symbol of spiritual fathers, the moon a symbol of spiritual mothers and the stars are a symbol of the children (sons).

> *[9] Then he dreamed still another dream and told it to his brothers, and said, "Look, I have dreamed another dream. And this time, the **sun**, the **moon**, and the **eleven stars** bowed down to me." [10] So he told it to his father and his brothers; and his father rebuked him and said to him, "What is this dream that you have dreamed? Shall your **mother** and **I** and **your brothers** indeed come to bow down to the earth before you?" **(Genesis 37:9-10).***

Joseph had a dream of the "sun," "moon" and "eleven stars" bowing to him. Jacob, Joseph's father, understood this to mean that he (Jacob, the sun), Joseph's mother (the moon), and Joseph's eleven brothers (the eleven stars) would one day have to "bow down" to Joseph. Thus, the sun can be a symbol of "fathers" in the ministry (1 Corinthians 4:15). The moon is symbolic of "mothers" in the ministry (1 Timothy 5:2); and/or the Church in general (compare Songs of Solomon 6:10). The stars are symbols of the children of the father and mother. With that said, "the stars of heaven" are also a representation of Abraham's seed—children (Hebrews 11:12). According to Paul in Romans 4:16, Abraham's seed includes those of the faith of Abraham.

Thus, a "great (mega) wind" can cause immature saints (stars or figs) to fall. Doctrine is like a mega wind; once it is taught, it can blow immature saints all over the place causing a "fallen" state. That is, a wind of doctrine can cause the immature seed of God (stars, figs) to fall. This fall is a direct result of no photosynthesis from the sun (fathers in the Church). Why?

"The sun became black (or dirty, black ink). If there is no sunlight, then the figs (stars) cannot mature. That is, if the leaders of the Church are "dirty," and stained with the "ink"[13] of unclean spirits, then the stars will remain immature and a great wind of false doctrine may cause them to fall. The wind was so severe that God had to stop the wind until He sealed some Israelites with His seal in their foreheads (Revelation 7).

> *¹After these things I saw four angels standing at the four corners of the earth, **holding the four winds** of the earth, that the **wind** should not blow on the earth, on the sea, or on any*

---

[13] According to 2 Corinthians 3:3 "ink" is also a symbol of "spirit."

> tree. ²*Then I saw another angel ascending from the east, having* **the seal** *of the living God. And he cried with a loud voice to the four angels to whom it was granted to harm the earth and the sea,* ³*saying, "Do not harm the earth, the sea, or the trees till we have sealed the servants of our God on their foreheads."*
> **(Revelation 7:1-3)**

The Spirit is the seal (Ephesians 1:13; 4:30). The wind can be symbolic of doctrines (Ephesians 5:14). Thus, they were sealed in their minds (foreheads) by the Spirit of the living God. That is, the living God imparted the mind of Christ to them by "engraving." using the "ink" of "the Spirit of the living God"

The same is true for all of Jesus' Church. Paul stated that the Church who receives the Holy Spirit is indeed sealed. The Holy Spirit is the seal! Paul declared in Ephesians 4:30, "And grieve not the Holy Spirit of God, whereby ye are sealed unto the day of redemption." This sealing occurred after the Ephesians "believed." Then, they "were sealed with the Holy Spirit of promise" (Ephesians 1:13).

We must first believe that Jesus is the Christ, and then in a separate experience, we are to be sealed with the Holy Spirit (Acts 19:1-7). Thus, the ultimate protection against "every wind of doctrine" is to have the seal of the Holy Spirit in one's forehead (mind). "Forehead" is the Greek compound "metopon" (**"mata,"** which means change, with, amidst, and **"ops,"** which means, eye, face).

Thus, the seal of the Spirit on their foreheads is the Spirit of the living God "changing" the way they "see" mentally that they might not be deceived by the mega wind of doctrine. Think of it, how many "mega wind (doctrine)" of today are deceiving people just because the preacher is "big" (vastly known, or rich)?

This seal in the forehead (a metaphor for the mind) is available for the believing Jews and believing Gentiles. Aaron, a type of Jesus has three "seals" on his high priest garments; he wore seals on his shoulder, his heart, and his forehead (Exodus 28). Jesus, our Great High Priest was also sealed of the Father (John 6:27).

Jesus was sealed on His shoulder when he was filled with the Holy Spirit at Jordan like the "onyx" stones were sealed on the shoulder of Aaron; that is, "the government will be upon His shoulder" (Exodus 28:9-12, NIV; Isaiah 9:6).

Jesus was sealed in His heart by water baptism[14] at the Jordan, like the sealed twelve stones worn on Aaron's heart (Exodus 28:21; 29). Thirdly, like Aaron wore the third and final seal on his forehead, Jesus was sealed in His forehead with the mind of the Father because Jesus is God's mind manifested.

Meaning, Jesus is God's "Logos" (a few of the definitions for "logos" is expressed thoughts, or exposed thoughts) (John 1; John 6:27). Yes, Jesus was the mind of God that walked the earth. If you want to know how the Father thinks, study Jesus' lifestyle. It follows that we are declared to also have the mind of Christ.

Paul declared in Ephesians 4:23, "be renewed in the spirit of your mind." Paul also declared in 1 Corinthians 2:15-16, "we have the mind of Christ," so that we can properly judge all things. The Spirit seals our minds by writing (engraving) the name (nature) of the Father and the Lamb in our foreheads (Revelation 14:1). He "changes" the way we "see" by engraving His fatherhood and the Lamb's nature into our minds.

---

[14] Water baptism is not only for washing away the filth of the flesh, but relates more to the human "conscience" (1 Peter 3:21); and the conscience relates to the heart (Hebrews 10:22).

"Clearly you are an epistle of Christ, ministered by us, written … by the Spirit of the living God … on tablets of flesh, that is, of the heart" (2 Corinthians 3:3). "Then I looked, and there before me was the Lamb, standing on Mount Zion, and with him 144,000 who had his name and his Father's name written on their foreheads" (Revelation 14:1, NIV). "Him that overcomes …I will write upon him the name of my God" (Revelation 3:12).

How to Know the Doctrines from God

John 7:17: If any man will do his will, he shall know of the doctrine, whether it be of God, or [whether] I speak of myself.

It appears that one of the most asked questions by the saints is: how does a person know whether a doctrine is from God? This is a legitimate question. In this season that we are living, there are many who have a doctrine that they "say" is from God. However, every doctrine that men/women claim is from God must be examined of in the light of Jesus' answer concerning knowing doctrines that are really from God. Here is Jesus' response to how to know doctrine that is from God.

> *14Now about the middle of the feast Jesus went up into the temple and taught. 15And the Jews marveled, saying, "How does this Man know letters, having never studied?" 16Jesus answered them and said, "My doctrine is not Mine, but His who sent Me. 17"**If anyone wants to do His will, he shall know concerning the doctrine, whether it is from God or whether I speak on My own authority.** 18"He who speaks from himself seeks his own glory; but He who seeks the glory of the One who sent Him is true, and no unrighteousness is in Him." (John 7:14-18).*

During the middle of the Feast of Tabernacles, Jesus went up into the temple and taught. His teaching was so profound that many "marveled," asking "how does this Man know letters, having never studied?" Like many today, some of the people of that day thought that formal "studying" at an establishment is the best way to learn and to teach doctrine. However, Jesus did not reference a formal education as the qualification to know doctrine. Jesus referenced God, the Father and "choosing God's choice," or "willing God's will," as the source of knowing doctrine.

In John 7:17 cited earlier, Jesus stated that **"if anyone wants to do His will, he shall know concerning the doctrine, whether it is from God."** Here is how that verse may also reads according to one of the definitions for the Greek word ("thelo" ("will")) translated as "want" and "will" in the New King James Version: "If anyone may **'choose'** to do **His 'choice,'** he shall know concerning the doctrine, whether it is from God;" or, "if anyone may **'desire'** to do **His 'desire,'** he shall know concerning the doctrine, whether it is from God;" or, "if anyone may **'prefer'** to do His **'preference,'** he shall know concerning the doctrine, whether it is from God;" or, "if anyone may **'delight'** to do His **'delight,'** he shall know concerning the doctrine, whether it is from God."

Thus, according to Jesus, to know God's doctrine, we must choose His choice, desire His desire, be pleased with His pleasure, prefer His preference, and will His will. The logical question is "What is God's choice, desire, will, pleasure, or preference, in order that I may know His doctrine?" Here are at least three articulations of God's will that are listed in the Scriptures that apply to all saints. These "will of God" may seem simplistic, yet they withstand strong winds of spurious doctrines.

God's will, choice, desire, preference for us is that we live sanctified (clean) life, abstaining from prostitution; that we give Him thanks "in everything" (note: God did not say we are to give Him thanks "for" everything;" but give Him thanks "in" every situation); and that we choose to accept His will for us to be "placed' (adopted) as "sons" of God.

> *For this is **the will** (lit., **thelo**) of God, your sanctification: that you should abstain from sexual immorality* **(1 Thessalonians 4:3-7).**
>
> *In everything give thanks; for this is **the will** (lit., **thelo**) of God in Christ Jesus for you* **(1 Thessalonians 5:18).**
>
> *Having predestined us to adoption as sons (lit., **son-placing**) by Jesus Christ to Himself, according to the good pleasure of **His will** (lit., **thelo**)"* **(Ephesians 1:5).**

If we choose God's choice as briefly outlined above, we will know the doctrine whether it is from God, or whether a doctrine was invented from humans. Saying it another way, some may have difficulty discerning the doctrines that are from God if they are not abstaining from fornication (sex outside of marriage, as defined by Jesus), if thanksgiving to God is not prevalent in their lives, and if they have not accepted His will for them to be "placed" as "mature sons," as Jesus was placed as "the Son of God."

With that said, here is another way that Jesus indicated that we can know the doctrine whether the doctrine is from God. Jesus taught if a person speaks from "his own" self by seeking his/her "own glory" and not the glory of Jesus and the glory of the heavenly Father, then his/her doctrine is not from God. "**For we do not preach ourselves, but Christ Jesus the Lord,** and ourselves your bondservants for Jesus' sake" (2 Corinthians 4:5). Saying it another way, if the doctrine is man centered, the doctrine is not from God.

The doctrine that is of God also has its source in God; that is, it must be from the heart of the Father concerning Jesus. Doctrines that are not from God may have their source from the Devil. In John 8:44, KJV, Jesus indicated that the Devil "speaks from his own," for he (the Devil) is a liar." The Devil is the opposite of Jesus. Jesus' doctrine comes from God, and not from His own self. **Our Lord Jesus declared that "I can of mine own self do nothing"** (John 5:30, KJV).

Jesus also stated in John 7:18 that "He who speaks from himself seeks his own glory." Thus, it is devilish to teach doctrine that glorifies one's own self. All doctrines that the ministers of Jesus teach are to be from God and must glorify Jesus, and should be Jesus centered, emphasizing Jesus, and not man-centered. Yet, there is an exception, if the preacher knows where he (the preacher) comes from.[15]

> *For we do not preach ourselves, but* **Christ Jesus the Lord,** *and ourselves your bondservants for Jesus' sake* **(2 Corinthians 4:5).**

> *But I make known to you, brethren that the gospel which was preached by me is* **not according to man (see Galatians 1:11).**

Thus, we can know if a doctrine is from God if we choose to do God's will (choice, desire, pleasure, etc.) for our lives; and the three references of the "will of God" listed previously, applies to all saints. With that's said, God's choice for us could also be a specific assignment (1 Corinthians 1:1; Ephesians 1:1). God's choice for us is also to suffer for Christ, even though we are doing what is right (1 Peter 3:17; 1 Peter 4:19). God's choice for us may be specifics with regards to giving as stipulated by the Holy Spirit and not by the dictates of man (2 Corinthians 8:5). God's choice for us may be to "serve" our generation like David did (Acts 13:36).

---

[15] Compare John 8:12-15

Jesus simplified the process by which we can know the doctrine that is from God. It is not complicated. All we have to do is choose to do His will and we will automatically "know" Jesus' doctrine as opposed to the different doctrines that exist today. And the Word of God has listed the "will of God" as set forth briefly in this chapter. I conclude this section with these verses:

> *You have an anointing from the Holy One, and you know all things (see 1 John 2:20).*
>
> *The anointing which you have received from Him abides in you, and you do not need that anyone teach you; but as **the same anointing teaches** you concerning all things, and is true, and is not a lie, and just as it has taught you, you will abide in Him (see 1 John 2:27).*

The "true" anointing who abides in us also teaches us; and because the anointing teaches us, pseudo doctrines cannot seduce us from God; because Jesus' anointing teaches us to "**'remain'** in Him (Jesus)."

Jesus' Doctrine of Vision

Habakkuk 2:2-3: *²And the LORD answered me, and said, Write the vision, and make [it] plain upon tables, that he may run that reads it. ³For the vision [is] yet for an appointed time, but at the end **'He'** shall speak, and not lie: though **'He'** tarry, wait for **'Him;'** because **'He'** will surely come, **'He'** will not tarry.*

Hebrews 10:37: *For yet a little while, and **He** that shall come will come, and will not tarry*

Jesus is the Vision as established by Habakkuk and confirmed in the Book of Hebrews. Jesus (the Word) also established the doctrine of His vision. The vision is simple. We must become like/as Jesus when He walked the earth almost 2,000 years ago. The vision of God is for us to conform to the image of His Son—Jesus (Romans 9:29). Yet, we hear so many variegated visions today that it becomes nauseating trying to keep up with every vision as established by the "commandments and doctrines of men." Jesus, on the other hand, gave the five-fold Christ gifts of apostles, prophets, evangelist, pastors, and teachers to establish His doctrine of vision in the Body of Christ.

The vision of Jesus is that "we all come to the 'oneness' of the faith ... of the Son of God," and that "we all come to the 'oneness' ... of the 'exact-knowledge'[16] of the Son of God." Coming to the same faith that Jesus has; and coming into the same exact knowledge that Jesus walked in, while on earth, are defined by the Bible as the Church (the Body of Christ) attaining to the "mature man."—a man of His love.

---

[16] The word "knowledge" (epi-gnosis) in Ephesians 4:13 is translated as "upon-knowledge" and is defined as "exact-knowledge," just as "epi-center" (upon-center) of an earthquake is defined as exact-center of the earthquakes.

This oneness with His faith and oneness with His knowledge is the vision of Jesus for His Church. He vision is summed up by Paul indicating that we are to grow into "the measure of the stature of the fullness of Christ." Simply put, the Father's vision for His Church is that we morph into the same image that Jesus characterized, through the same filling of the Holy Spirit that Jesus received. Here is the Apostle Paul's vision statement, or his doctrine of vision.

> [11]*And He Himself gave some to be apostles, some prophets, some evangelists, and some pastors and teachers,* [12]*for the equipping of the saints for the work of ministry, for the edifying of the body of Christ,* [13]***till we all come to the unity of the faith and of the knowledge of the Son of God, to a perfect man, to the measure of the stature of the fullness of Christ;*** [14]*that we should no longer be children, tossed to and fro and carried about with every wind of doctrine, by the trickery of men, in the cunning craftiness of deceitful plotting,* [15]*but, speaking the truth in love, may grow up in all things into Him who is the head – Christ –* [16]*from whom the whole body, joined and knit together by what every joint supplies, according to the effective working by which every part does its share, causes growth of the body for the edifying of itself in love* **(Ephesians 4:11-16).**

Paul preached Jesus' vision. Jesus' vision is that "all" of "we" gain the same faith that the Son of God—Jesus—attained. Jesus' vision is that "we all" attain the same exact knowledge that Jesus, the Son of God attained. Jesus' vision of the believers having the same faith and same exact knowledge of the Son of God is summed up as "we all" becoming that "perfect (lit., mature) man"—a man of His love. Or, "we all" attaining to the same faith of Jesus and the same exact knowledge of Jesus is also summed as us attaining to "the measure of the 'adult age' of the 'filling' of Christ" — which also includes, the filling of God's love that passes knowledge.

Whew! I get pleasure just writing about the possibilities that will manifest through the filling of the Holy Spirit when we reach the same measure that Jesus did in His "prime," expressing God's faith and God's knowledge through the Spirit given to Jesus without measure. So, what doctrine did Paul give us to enable us to reach the same faith and the same exact knowledge of Jesus? Paul set it forth in the Scriptures cited earlier.

The first step is that Jesus gave, as gifts to the Body of Christ, apostles, prophets, evangelist, pastors, and teachers to facilitate His vision. These gifts were given to the Church "until."

So, the obvious question is, "until when?"

And the obvious answer is, until we all come to the unity (lit., oneness) of the same faith that Jesus had and oneness with the same exact-knowledge that Jesus had. Here is the big question, have all the Body of Christ come to the same faith that Jesus demonstrated? The obvious answer is, no! Or, does all the Body of Christ possesses the same exact-knowledge that Jesus exemplified? The answer is not yet!

Therefore, Ephesians 4:11 states that Jesus **"in fact"**[17] gave apostles, prophets, evangelists, pastors and teachers to the Body of Christ "until" the Church grows into the "mature man," "until" the Church is able to contain the same immeasurable "filling" of the Holy Spirit that Jesus was able to contain in the temple of His body.

---

[17] See Greek texts

The second step to attaining the same faith and the exact knowledge that Jesus envisioned for His Church is accomplished as the five-fold ministry (apostles, prophets, evangelist, teachers, and pastors) apply the three phases of development of the saints of God.

*He Himself gave some to be apostles, some prophets, some evangelists, and some pastors and teachers, for the **equipping** of the saints for **the work of ministry, for the edifying of the body of Christ** (Ephesians 4:11-12).*

Once a person becomes a believer, the vision of Christ for that person should be to first **equip** him/her. Second, encourage that believer to do the **work** of ministry. Third, that person should **be edified and in turn that person edifies** the Body of Christ. Let us look at all three phases separately and briefly.

1. The word **"equipping"** and its associated root word and inflections are translated in the Bible as "mending," "restoring," "perfectly joined," perfect, frame, etc. (Strong's NT: #2677, #2675). They are defined as: to fully qualify, adjust, fully prepare, repair, arrange, and so on. Thus, when a person receives Jesus salvation, the five-fold ministry first order of business is to mend, restore, and furnish what is needed to that saint. The word is used with respect to the disciples "mending" their nets when Jesus called them (Matthew 4:21). It is also used for how God "framed" the ages with His Word (Hebrews 11:3). It is used of the saints being "perfectly joined together in the same mind and in the same 'knowing" (see 1 Corinthians 1:10). The five-fold ministry is to use the Word of God to frame, mend and equip the

saints of the living God. The saints are to be framed into the body of Christ as God as set them.

2. The **"work of the ministry"** involves the same work that Jesus did; the same type of work that Paul, Peter, John, James, Philip, Mary, Junia, Timothy, Epaphroditus, and so on performed. We are to pray, study God's Word, evangelize, heal the sick, cast out demons, raise the dead, and cleanse the leper, etc.

3. **"Edifying"** is defined as building up, "home-building, etc. Thus, the five-fold ministry is to also give understanding to the saints of the living God that they are indeed the "house of God." The five-fold ministry must encourage the saints of God to build up each other, to build their homes and family in the name of our Lord Jesus Christ. We edify each other and ourselves through the prophetic. According to Paul, we edify through authority, we edify through praying in the Holy Spirit, and so on.

So, in the three items above we see Jesus' doctrine of His vision for His Church taking shape. The Church must accept the five gifts of apostles, prophets, evangelist, pastors, and teachers given to the Church to fully experience the three phases of being mended/equipped, working in the ministry and edification. The purpose of Jesus mending us, the purpose of us doing the work of the ministry, and the purpose of edification is to bring all of us to the same faith of God that Jesus walked in and the same exact knowledge that Jesus possessed. Why? So, we can walk in the same measure of faith and knowledge that Jesus walked in while he was on the earth. Here are examples of "the faith of the Son of God" and "the exact-knowledge" that Jesus demonstrated.

We must first understand that the "faith of the Son of God" is synonymous with the "faith of God" or the "God kind of faith." Jesus demonstrated this faith of God—the faith of the Son of God—during His second purging of the temple (Matthew 21; Mark 11; Luke 19). During this time Jesus cursed a fig tree for not producing fruit for Him when the Son of God walked by the tree. The disciples became astonished that the fig tree that Jesus cursed[18] withered so quickly. Jesus replied by saying, "Have faith in God (Mark 11:22). The Greek structure for this phrase, literally reads, **"Have the faith of God."**

This "God kind of faith" is the ability of a believer to believe that those things which a believer "says" and "does not doubt in his heart, but believes that those things he **says** will be done; he will have whatever he says" (Mark 11:23). Paul also stated that he lived his life by the faith **of** the Son of God in Galatians 2:20. "I have been crucified with Christ; it is no longer I who live, but Christ lives in me; and the life which I now live in the flesh **I live by faith in the Son of God,** who loved me and gave Himself for me." We are living because of His (Jesus') faith; therefore, Jesus' vision is that we walked in the full maturity of the faith of the Son of God—Jesus. That is, walking in "His faith" is part of what it means to walk in the finish work of Jesus.

An example of Jesus' exact-knowledge is demonstrated in the prophetic with the woman at the well in John 4. The Bible says that" mature love" enables a person to **"know even as they are**

---

[18] An answer to the question why Jesus cursed the tree when it was not the time of figs could be understood in this. The Father created the earth and all that is in her to also provide for God's sons. It appears to me "the day" and the earth should have recognized that Jesus, the Son of God "was hungry" and should have produced figs for Him automatically (compare Matthew 6:34). If Jesus had not expected the fig three to have produced the fruits for Him, He would not have looked for figs or cursed the tree for not producing figs.

known" (1 Corinthians 13: 10-12 w/1 Corinthians 13:1-9). Jesus is the love of God demonstrated. Thus, Jesus walked in exact-knowledge because of His mature love. His knowledge was not just accurate[19] knowledge, but He walked in exact-knowledge. When Jesus met the woman at the well in John 4, He was able to tell her "exactly" her entire life through the demonstration of exact-knowledge that flows through love (see John 4:29; 1 Corinthians 13:10-12). The woman got so excited that she eventually went to her hometown and evangelized. This is what she said, "Come, see a Man who **told me all things that I ever did**. Could this be the Christ?" Jesus' vision for His Church is to also walk in the same exact-knowledge as the Son of God.[20]

With all that said, it appears to me that ministers of the gospel have convoluted the vision of Jesus for His Church. Men have also invented many so-called visions that came out of their own hearts. Let us keep the vision for the Church simple as Paul, Peter, James, John, and the rest of the early apostles did. Let us now bear the image of the Last Adam—Jesus.

---

[19] If we perform a math problem and get an answer of $\sqrt{2}$, this is an "exact" answer; however, if I simplify $\sqrt{2}$, the answer becomes 1. 4142, which then becomes an "accurate" answer; yet it is not the exact answer. As indicated earlier we can walk in the "exact" way of God (Acts 18:26).
[20] Compare Jeremiah 9:24, Galatians 4:1-9

Doctrine of Purpose

2 Timothy 1:9: *Who has saved us, and called [us] with a holy calling, not according to our works, but according to **his own purpose** and grace, which was **given us in Christ Jesus** before the world began.*

Jesus' purpose for mankind is preeminent over all others so called purposes in this life. God's purpose was "given us in Christ Jesus before 'times ages'." The word "purpose," in the New Testament is defined as "pre-placed." That is, our purpose in this life is what God, the Father, has "pre-placed" for us to become. Another synonym for purpose is "predestined" or "predestination."

One of the definitions for "predestine" in the Greek New Testament is "pre-defined," "foreordained," pre-specify, to set a "prior-boundary," etc. The Word of God defines God's "purpose" or "predestination" for our lives as: **"to be conformed to the image of His Son ...."** Another of God's **"purpose of the ages"** is that we **"make known His manifold wisdom"** to **"all,"** including, but not limited, to principalities and authorities in the heavenly places.

We should not replace the purposes of God (i.e. believers being conformed into the image of His Son, Jesus) with humanistic purposes (i.e. seeking to conform to the world's images of the beast system). The foremost purpose for our lives as defined in the Romans 8 is to be **"placed as mature sons through Jesus Christ;"** that is we are to be **"'morphed' into the image of His Son,"** Jesus Christ. The same image that Jesus is, we are to become and bear. This is our purpose in life. Here is God's purpose statement for us:

> ^{28}*And we know that all things work together for good to those who love God, to those who are the called according to His* **purpose.** ^{29}*For whom He foreknew, He also* **predestined** *to be conformed to the image of His Son, that He might be the firstborn among many brethren* (**Romans 8:28-29**)

There are so many frustrated people attempting to find their so-called purpose; and if truth be told, the purpose they are looking for is a job that will make them lots of money, without any hard work. The purpose of God (to be conformed to the image of Jesus) has been replaced with humanistic purposes (i.e. a job that enables "conspicuous consumption").

Yet, if you are indeed interested in finding your "purpose job," Solomon in Ecclesiastes 3:1 uses the word "purpose" with respect to those who live "under the sun." The Strong's Concordance defines **"purpose"** as that which you are **"inclined to do"** with an element of **"pleasure"** in this purpose. Thus, your purpose as it relates to a job may be linked to something legal and right that you are **"happy"** performing. Solomon also taught that **"whatever**[21] your hand finds to do, do it with your might ..." (Ecclesiastes 9:10).

With that said, the truth of God's purpose that we should bear the image of Jesus, first, still stands! We can then allow the sovereign God to **"add"** to us the reward and blessings of our father Abraham. Jesus said we cannot "serve God and 'riches'" (Matthew 6:24). Jesus also taught that we must become rich towards God, foremost (Luke 12: 21; Matthew 6:33-34). Jesus also made clear the pathway to receive a hundredfold (riches) and inherit eternal like in Matthew 19:23-30.

---

[21] Note: the Hebrew word "AShR" is also translated as "happy."

God is not against riches or the rich, God has a problem with those who "trust in riches," or "uncertain riches" and are not rich towards God (Luke 12:21; Mark 10:24; 1 Timothy 6:17). According to the New Testament, there are two main purposes of God. We are to become mature believers to be "placed" as His "sons" and daughters; and we are to make known His many-colored wisdom to all, including, but not limited to principalities and powers in the heavens; and God's purposes must become preeminent in our lives.

> ³*Blessed be the God and Father of our Lord Jesus Christ, who has blessed us with every spiritual blessing in the heavenly places in Christ,* ⁴***just as He chose us in*** *Him before the foundation of the world, that we should be holy and without blame before Him in love,* ⁵***having predestined us to adoption as sons by Jesus Christ to Himself,*** *according to the good pleasure of His will,* ⁶*to the praise of the glory of His grace, by which He has made us accepted in the Beloved* **(Ephesians 1:3-6).**
>
> ⁸*To me, who am less than the least of all the saints, this grace was given, that I should preach among the Gentiles the unsearchable riches of Christ,* ⁹*and to make all see what is the fellowship of the mystery, which from the beginning of the ages has been hidden in God who created all things through Jesus Christ;* ¹⁰***to the intent*** *that now the* ***manifold wisdom of God*** *might be made known by the church to the principalities and powers in the heavenly places,* ¹¹*according to the* ***eternal purpose*** *which He accomplished in Christ Jesus our Lord* **(Ephesians 3:8-11).**

God, the Father, works all things "according to the counsel of **His will."** It is not our so-called purposes that become preeminent. It is His "pre-placed" purposes and His "predetermined" destiny that matters. He has purposed us to be "placed"[22] as "mature sons" just as He placed Jesus as the mature Son. We must wear the same image that Jesus wore by having the same faith[23] that Jesus had, and having the same knowledge[24] that Jesus possessed when He walked the earth in the flesh. Again, we are purposed to be placed as sons having Jesus' image. This is the same image and purpose that Jesus had when He walked the earth and after His resurrection!

> *[28]And we know that all things work together for good to those who love God, to those who are the called according to His **purpose**. [29]For whom He foreknew, **He also predestined to be conformed to the image of His Son**, that He might be the firstborn among many brethren* **(Romans 8:28-29)**.

Another purpose of God is that "the 'variegated' wisdom of God might be made known by the church to the principalities and powers in the heavenly places, according to the **'purpose of the ages'** which He accomplished in Christ Jesus our Lord" (Ephesians 3:10-11). This manifold wisdom is to show these principalities and authorities in the heavenly dimensions that God, the Father, can indeed use the Church to save heathens through the preaching of the cross of Jesus Christ. To some of us, the heathen nations may seem unredeemable because of their heathen practices as taught by principalities and authorities.

However, God's "purpose of the ages" (God's manifold wisdom manifesting by the coming of Jesus Christ as the Son of the living God, as Savior, as Baptizer, as King, as Lord, and the establishing of the true Church to continue what Jesus implemented through

---

[22] I have developed this topic in one of my other books, titled, *The Days of the Seventh Angel*.
[23] Galatians 2:20
[24] 1 Corinthians 13:10 w/1 Corinthians 13:12

the cross) surpasses any heathen practices that may have a hold on humanity. Now, I am not saying that preaching Jesus in the nations with the view to end the work of principalities and authorities in their lives is easy; yet, one of God's purposes, in indeed, for us is to be conformed to the image of Jesus Christ so that we may be placed as mature sons to do the same great works in the nations, as Jesus commissioned.

Part of God's purposes is for the Church to make known God's many-colored wisdom to the authorities of darkness by using the wisdom of the preaching of the cross of Jesus Christ to save as many as we can. Heathenism or atheism is not stronger than God. Neither principalities, authorities nor mankind are wiser than God. The gospel of Christ is also the power of God (Romans 1:16).

In other words, there is nothing that principalities can "begin" in humans that God cannot recover them out-of through the cross, blood, baptism, and Spirit of Jesus. There are no false authorities established in humans that Jesus cannot overcome with His identity in them. The Word of God says that **"the foolishness of God is wiser than men, and the weakness of God is stronger than men (1 Corinthians 1:25).**

Proverbs 21:30: There is no wisdom or understanding or counsel against the Lord.

Paul said that God "saved us and called us … according to His **own** purpose and grace which was **given to us in Christ Jesus** before time began" (2 Timothy 1:9). God's purpose is for us to be conformed to the same image as Jesus. This purpose is "given to us in Christ Jesus." God's purpose is for Himself ("His own purpose"), not for any humanistic,[25] misplaced purpose.

God's purpose is for us to preach His wisdom (Jesus and Him crucified) to the unsaved that they might have the same access as we have to the Father through the Holy Spirit (Ephesians 2:18). Jesus stripped principalities and powers and all handwriting of laws that were contrary to the heathens has been removed by the cross of Christ (Colossians 2:14-15). All can be forgiven and delivered by Jesus through preaching the death, burial, and resurrection of Jesus (1 Timothy 2:4).

It is our work to fulfill God's purpose of preaching the power of God, the cross of Jesus, so that humanity may accept Jesus as their Savior, King, Lord, Baptizer, etc. It is God's purpose that we be placed as mature sons, just as Jesus was placed as the mature Son. One of the "spiritual blessings" we have "in the heavenly places in Christ" is that "he chose us in Him … having **predestined** us to **'sons-placing'**[26] by Jesus Christ to Himself" (Ephesians 1:3-5).

---

[25] Man-centered

[26] "Adoption as sons" literally means "to be placed as a mature son;" again, for further development, refer to one of my other books, *The Days of the Seventh Angel.*

Doctrine of Duality

Jesus marginalized Satan; and the Church is to do the same. We should not focus on the Devil. In this age, ministers preach more about Satan than they do God. All of God's ministers need to preach a **mega God** and less and less about Satan. The doctrine of dualism[27] preaches a great God; and then, in the same breath, emphasizes the Devil. All the Church and the world need to know that God is in control, not the Devil.

Preachers need to declare the Kinship and Lordship of Jesus. If they are going to mention the Devil, declare how weak he is to Jesus and Jesus' blood. The Bible contains about three-quarters of a million words to nine hundred thousand words, depending on the translation. Satan and his associated names are mentioned significantly less than 0. 001% of the time. If God marginalizes the tempter in His Word, so should the Church.

Satan has nothing in Jesus! Jesus bound Satan! Jesus judged Satan! Jesus cast Satan out of this world! Michael, the arch angel cast Satan out of heaven because Satan is not strong enough to tangle with Michael! The blood of Jesus overcomes Satan. The blood of Jesus is a boundary Satan and his angels cannot pass! Do you know that Satan is subjected to Jesus and His apostles? Preachers need to stop teaching an imbalanced doctrine concerning Satan.

Satan has nothing (not one thing) in Jesus! Jesus declared, *"I will no longer talk much with you, for the ruler of this world is coming, and he has nothing in Me"* (John 14:30).

---

[27] A term used by my spiritual father, Dr Kelley Varner

Jesus bound Satan! ²⁶*"If Satan casts out Satan, he is divided against himself. How then will his kingdom stand? ²⁷And if I cast out demons by Beelzebub, by whom do your sons cast them out? Therefore, they shall be your judges. ²⁸But if I cast out demons by the Spirit of God, surely the kingdom of God has come upon you. ²⁹Or how can one enter a strong man's house and plunder his goods, unless he first **binds** the strong man? And then he will plunder his house"* (Matthew 12:26-29). Jesus **bound** Satan and plunders his house by casting out demons from the bodies of some folks.

Satan is judged! ⁷*"Nevertheless I tell you the truth ... the Helper ... I will send Him to you. ⁸And when He has come, He will convict the world ... ¹¹**of judgment,** because the ruler of this world **is judged.** (John 16:7-11)*

Jesus cast Satan out of this world! ³⁰*"Jesus answered and said, "This voice did not come because of Me, but for your sake. ³¹"**Now** is the judgment of this world; **now** the ruler of this world will be cast out"* (John 12:30-31).

Michael, the arch angel cast Satan out of heaven, because Satan is "not strong enough" to tangle with Michael! ⁷*"And there was war in heaven. Michael and his angels fought against the dragon, and the dragon and his angels fought back. ⁸But he was not **strong enough,** and they lost their place in heaven. ⁹The great dragon was hurled down — that ancient serpent called the devil, or Satan, who leads the whole world astray. He was hurled to the earth, and his angels with him."* (Revelation 12:7-9, NIV).

Jesus, the "stronger than he (Satan)," stripped Satan of his amour (his strength) (Luke 11:19-22). Since Jesus stripped Satan of the armor of his strength, Satan is "not strong enough" any longer. Thus, Michael was able so defeat Satan, because the Devils is "not strong enough" to prevail.

The blood of Jesus overcomes Satan! *⁹"So the great dragon was cast out, that serpent of old, called the Devil and Satan, who deceives the whole world; he was cast to the earth, and his angels were cast out with him. ¹⁰Then I heard a loud voice saying in heaven, now salvation, and strength, and the kingdom of our God, and the power of His Christ have come, for the accuser of our brethren, who accused them before our God day and night, has been cast down.* **¹¹And they overcame him by the blood of the Lamb** *and by the word of their testimony, and they did not love their lives to the death" (Revelation 12:9-11).* As the Philistines in 1 Samuel 17 could not pass "Ephes Dammin" ("boundary of bloods"), so Satan is overcome by the blood of the Lamb. **In the blood of Jesus, you are protected!**

Jesus subjected Satan to Him and to Jesus' apostles! *²¹"There is also an antitype which now saves us – baptism (not the removal of the filth of the flesh, but the answer of a good conscience toward God),* **through the resurrection of Jesus Christ,** *²²who has gone into heaven and is at the right hand of God,* **angels and authorities and powers** *having been made* **subject** *to Him" (1 Peter 3:21-22).* Paul declared that he had authority to deliver blasphemers to be disciplined by Satan *"of whom are Hymenaeus and Alexander, whom* **I delivered to Satan that they may learn not to blaspheme"** *(see 1 Timothy 1:20).* In other words, Satan and his angels are also subjected to apostles. (1 Timothy 1:20; 2 Corinthians 5:1-5).

Jesus is the head of all principalities and powers and He "triumphed" over them on the cross. That is, Jesus stripped and disarmed Satan and all his angels; and Jesus paraded them naked in chains and made a public spectacle of them. The house of Jesus is waxing stronger and stronger, and Satan and his angels are weaker and weaker!

⁸Beware lest anyone cheat you through philosophy and empty deceit, according to the tradition of men, according to the basic *principles of the world, and not according to Christ. ⁹For in Him dwells all the fullness of the Godhead bodily; ¹⁰and you are complete in Him, who is **the head** of all principality and power. ¹¹In Him you were also circumcised with the circumcision made without hands, by putting off the body of the sins of the flesh, by the circumcision of Christ, ¹²buried with Him in baptism, in which you also were raised with Him through faith in the working of God, who raised Him from the dead. ¹³And you, being dead in your trespasses and the uncircumcision of your flesh, He has made alive together with Him, having forgiven you all trespasses, ¹⁴having wiped out the handwriting of requirements that was against us, which was contrary to us. And He has taken it out of the way, having nailed it to the cross. ¹⁵Having **disarmed** principalities and powers, He made a public spectacle of them, **triumphing over them in it** (Colossians 2:8-15).*

The Doctrine of Self-Appointments

Jeremiah 23:21: I have not sent these prophets, yet they ran: I have not spoken to them, yet they prophesied.

There are many today who are calling themselves from themselves. They are "prophets from their own hearts." Some are like Jezebel, as stated in the book of Revelation, who "calls herself a prophetess." God "have not sent these prophets." This generation really must be prayerful with respect to going into the ministry. This generation must allow God to initiate His calling for their lives, versus self-appointment.

*¹For every high priest taken from among men is appointed for men in things pertaining to God, that he may offer both gifts and sacrifices for sins. ²He can have compassion on those who are ignorant and going astray, since he himself is also subject to weakness. ³Because of this he is required as for the people, so also for himself, to offer sacrifices for sins. ⁴And **no man takes this honor to himself,** but he who is **called by God,** just as Aaron was. ⁵So also Christ did not glorify Himself to become High Priest, but it was He who said to Him: "You are My Son, Today I have begotten You." ⁶As He also says in another place: "You are a priest forever According to the order of Melchizedek"* **(Hebrews 5:1-6)**

Jesus was not self-appointed: God called him. "And **no man takes this honor to himself,** but he who is **called by God**, just as Aaron was. **So also, Christ did not glorify Himself** to become High Priest, but it was He who said to Him: "You are My Son, Today I have begotten You." The Lord is very vocal about self-appointed ministers and ministers who are appointed by unauthorized men and women. Here are some of the Scriptures.

> *"They set up kings, but not by Me; They made princes, but I did not acknowledge them ..."* **(Hosea 8:4).**

There are many "kings" (leaders) being "set up" in the Body of Christ; but it is not by God, neither does God acknowledge them. Jeroboam did something similar. **"He made shrines (lit., houses) on the high places, and made priests from every class[28] of people, who were not of the sons of Levi"** (1 Kings 12:31). "Shrines" (manmade buildings) and priests from a class of people who are not of the sons of Jesus are being installed as ministers. This is being done by some preacher because of insecurities to hold people in the name of maintaining people.

> *"The priests did not say, 'Where is the LORD?' And those who handle the law did not know Me; the rulers also transgressed against Me; the prophets prophesied by Baal, and walked after things that do not profit"* (Jeremiah 2:8).

Jeremiah gave one of the qualifications to handle the Law (the Word of God). Ministers must "know" the Lord. Ministers must not prophesy in the wrong spirit (Baal[29]). Ministers must not walk after things that do not cause them to profit (lit., ascend). The qualification is not necessarily how much knowledge one has, but whether a person knows the One who has all knowledge. In Jeremiah 5:31, he declared that **"the prophets prophesy falsely,** and the **priests rule by their own power;** and **My people love to have it so.** But what will you do in the end?" Yes! Some of God's people love false prophets; some of God's people love priests who rule by their own means! Ezekiel also spoke about those who became **"prophets from their own**

---

[28] The Hebrew word for "every class" literally means "extremity;" therefore these people appointed by men will dogmatically teach "extreme" doctrines with no balance in their teachings.
[29] Jesus defined Baal as Satan (Matthew 12:24-26)

hearts." That is, they follow their own spirits and did **not** see or hear anything from God.

"And the word of the LORD came to me, saying, ²Son of man, prophesy against the prophets of Israel who prophesy, and say to **those who prophesy out of their own heart,** *Hear the word of the LORD! ³Thus says the Lord GOD: Woe to the foolish prophets, who follow their own spirit and have seen nothing" (Ezekiel 13:1-3)!*

The phrase "those who prophesy out of their own hearts" literally reads in the Hebrew text as **"those who are prophets from their own hearts."** It appears to me that every minister of the gospel who believes they are called should seek the Lord to make sure they did not make themselves prophets from their own hearts. I know the Lord Jesus will speak to them to confirm whether they are called or not. Jeremiah 17:9 said that the heart is deceitful above all things, and desperately wicked. Who can know it? **Thus, those who are seeking to be ministers must not take the honor of ministry on themselves by themselves, from themselves.** If they are not sons of Jesus, they should not force their way into the ministerial priesthood.[30]

"Then His disciples came and said to Him, "Do You know that the Pharisees were offended when they heard this saying?" ¹³But He answered and said, **"Every plant which My heavenly Father has not planted will be uprooted"**" (Matthew 15:12-13). Here is the question: Did the Father plant you as a leader? If you are not sure, seek the Lord again, and again, and again to make sure; He will give you an answer of peace.

---

[30] I understand that all believers are priest unto God (1 Peter 2:9, Revelation 5:1); however, there is also the priesthood of the five-fold ministry. That is, in Romans 15:16 when Paul referred to him being a "minister of Jesus Christ," he called it "ministering," which is literally "priest-working."

I remember once, I was meditating on Ezekiel 13 for a few days. When I discovered how the Hebrew actually reads in Ezekiel 13:2 — that some are "prophets from their own hearts," — I immediately cried out, **again, and again** to the Lord to make sure I was not in that class of apostles or prophets who became apostles or prophets "from their own hearts;" and He answered me! The Lord Jesus said to me that evening in a clear voice that was still, sweet, and pleasant to my ears and spirit, He said **"it is not so with you my-son."** My spirit rejoiced at the sound and taste of His words. God will give you an answer of peace. (I am not sure how your heart is before the Lord, but I fear Him enough not to play with His calling.)

Yet, here is another side of what can happen to those who call themselves and send themselves. A few years back, a false prophet came to our Church, during one of our seminars, who began to have "diarrhea of the mouth,"[31] and he was putting down the work the Lord gave our Church to complete. (The reason as to why he felt he had to speak against us is too long to include in this book). The false prophet became so violent against me he wanted to physically harm me. That following Sunday, I indicated to our Church that God did not send that false prophet and that he had to be careful what he spoke against our ministry. I also explicitly said that that prophet had to be careful what he said because the Lord would remove him from the earth for saying "God says" if God did not speak to him to say. Within a year or so that prophet died. (Compare Jeremiah 28 when a false prophet died within seven months after prophesying lies to God's people, compare Ezekiel 11:13). False prophets must be careful when they prophesy lies saying the Lord says and the Lord did not say.

---

[31] Dr. Kelley Varner used this euphemism at times.

Jeremiah and Ezekiel clearly state that one of the main things that makes a prophet false is for that prophet to say, the Lord told me to say such and such, and the Lord did not really speak to them. Jeremiah 23:21 says, "I have not sent these prophets, yet they ran. **I have not spoken to them, yet they prophesied."**

Jeremiah 23:31 says, "Behold, I am against the prophets," says the LORD, "who use their tongues and say, 'He says.'" Ezekiel 13:6-7 says, "They have envisioned futility and false divination, saying, 'Thus says the LORD!' But the LORD has not sent them; yet they hope that the word may be confirmed. Have you not seen a futile vision, and have you not spoken false divination? **You say, 'The LORD says,' but I have not spoken."**

Please note that I am not writing this chapter to discourage ministers from entering the work of the Lord. Jesus said that the harvest is plenty; however, the laborers are few. What is being encouraged is that everyone who claims to be an apostle, prophet, teacher, evangelist, or pastor makes sure they are indeed called and chosen by God to the offices they are occupying. And make sure God does indeed speak to you before you say, "God says." May the Lord Jesus be with your spirit!

The Doctrine of the "Rapture"

It appears to me that one of the most misunderstood topics is the physical return ("coming") of our Lord Jesus from heaven. Ministers cannot seem to agree on **the "times and seasons" (plural)**[32] **concerning His coming!** Men have invented doctrinal phrases like **"the rapture" "pre-tribulation rapture," "mid-tribulation rapture," "post-tribulation rapture"** to predict the times and seasons of Jesus' coming. There is also confusion and fear with regards to the "great tribulation."

The book of Revelation teaches that the "great tribulation" started some 2,000 years ago. Yet, tribulation is a part of the Christian life until Jesus returns (1 Thessalonians 3:3-4, Revelation 13:9). There is also no such word as "rapture" in the Bible. If you were to look up the word "rapture" in the Bible or is not found in the Bible.

I must also add that the apostle Peter made it clear that this subject is indeed a difficult subject[33] to understand; and I have personally gone back and forth on this issue of His coming until the Lord gave me rest concerning this. Thus, through reverence for the Lord Jesus, we must aspire to teach biblical doctrines concerning the "times and seasons" of Jesus' coming, "the great tribulation" and the end; and because of reverence to Jesus we must be willing to change our doctrine once our understanding increases, since some understanding the Lord Jesus gives is progressive.

The Bible does give us a hint of the "times and seasons" of His coming. Yes, we can know the times and season of Jesus' coming.

---

[32] 1 Thessalonians 5:1
[33] 2 Peter 3:16

However, please **note that** the Lord does come "as a thief" only to those in darkness (1 Thessalonians 5:2-4; Revelation 16:12-16). It was also **not** given to us to predict the exact day or hour of Jesus' coming (Matthew 24:36, Mark 13:32). It is foolish to predict the exact date (year, month, and day) of Jesus' coming. However, the sons of light are given to know the exact the times (plural) and seasons (plural).

> *¹But concerning the **times and the seasons**, brethren, you have no need that I should write to you. ²For you yourselves know **'exactly'** that the day of the Lord so comes as a thief in the night. ³For when they say, "Peace and safety!" then sudden destruction comes upon them, as labor pains upon a pregnant woman. And they shall not escape. ⁴**But you, brethren, are not in darkness, so that this Day should overtake you as a thief.** ⁵You are all sons of light and sons of the day. We are not of the night nor of darkness* **(1 Thessalonians 5:1-4)**.

Note Jesus coming is plural ("times" and "seasons"). With that said, one of the hints of the times and seasons of Jesus' coming is found in the most unlikely book of the Bible. I say the most unlikely book because the apostle that wrote the book was not necessarily a scholar like Paul. This apostle's name is Peter. Peter said, "For we have not followed cunningly devised fables, when we made known unto you the power and **coming of our Lord Jesus Christ,** but were eyewitnesses of his majesty" (2 Peter 1:16, KJV).

The next logical question is: when did Peter see the coming of our Lord Jesus? The answer is seen in 2 Peter 1:18. Peter equated the coming of the Lord Jesus to his experience with the Lord Jesus in the holy mountain (also known as the "mount of transfiguration") when Jesus was transfigured and God spoke to Jesus. Let us look at the verses.

> ¹⁶*For we have not followed cunningly devised fables, when we made known unto you the **power and coming of our Lord Jesus Christ**, but were **eyewitnesses** of his majesty.* ¹⁷*For he received from God the Father honor and glory, when there came such a voice to him from the excellent glory, this is my beloved Son, in whom I am well pleased.* ¹⁸*And this voice which came from heaven we heard, **when we were with him in the holy mount** (2 Peter 1:16-18).*

Let us go through the verses again for clarity. In 2 Peter 1:16, Peter declared that he made known to the people he was writing to "the power **and coming** of our Lord Jesus Christ," and that he was an **"eyewitness" of this coming.** In the subsequent verses of 2 Peter 1:18, Peter explained that he and the others two apostles saw "the power **and coming** of our Lord Jesus Christ" when they **"were with him in the holy mount."**

This was the same time that Peter also said that he heard God's voice speak to Jesus in this same holy mount. Thus, 2 Peter 2:16-18, provides explicit understanding concerning the coming of the Lord Jesus Christ. Peter was able to **"make known"** unto the saints he was writing to the power **and coming** of the Lord Jesus.

Thus, **we** can also **"know"** the power **and coming** of the Lord. How can the saints of today "know" the power and coming of the Lord Jesus Christ? We can know the power and coming of the Lord Jesus Christ by looking at the same event that Peter "saw" and "heard."

In other words, from the experience on the mountain where Jesus was transfigured, we can know as Peter made known to the Church, the Lord's coming. Let us read, for comparison, Matthew, Mark, and Luke's accounts with Peter's account of the same experience of the coming of our Lord Jesus Christ.

*16:28Verily I say unto you, there be some standing here, which shall not taste of death, till they **see the Son of man coming in his kingdom** ... 2... And was transfigured before them ... 5... a bright cloud overshadowed them: and behold a voice out of the cloud, which said, this is my beloved Son, in whom I am well pleased; hear you him* **(Matthew 16:28-17:1-5).**

*1And he said unto them, Verily I say unto you, that there be some of them that stand here, which shall not taste of death, till they have **seen the kingdom of God come** with power ... and he was transfigured before them ... 7And there was a cloud that overshadowed them: and a voice came out of the cloud, saying, this is my beloved Son: hear him* **(Mark 9:1-7).**

*27But I tell you of a truth, there be some standing here, which shall not taste of death, **till they see the kingdom of God** ... And as he prayed, the fashion of his countenance was altered, and ...34While he thus spoke, there came a cloud, and overshadowed them ...35And there came a voice out of the cloud, saying, this is my beloved Son: hear him* **(Luke 9:27-35).**

*16For we have not followed cunningly devised fables, when we made known unto you the power and **coming of our Lord Jesus Christ**, but were eyewitnesses of his majesty. 17 For he received from God the Father honor and glory, when there came such a voice to him from the excellent glory, this is my beloved Son, in whom I am well pleased. 18 And this voice which came from heaven we heard, when we were with him in the holy mount* **(2 Peter 1:16-18).**

Peter's account is the same as Matthew, Mark, and Luke's. They documented Jesus transfigured (Jesus became gloried before the eyes of Peter, James, and John), as Moses and Elijah also appeared with Jesus "in glory" (Luke 9:31). This transfiguration of Jesus (Jesus' gloried state) is what Peter called Jesus'

"coming." In Matthew's account Jesus Himself called His transfiguration "the Son of Man **coming** in His kingdom."

Peter said that "we (Peter, James and John) heard" God's voice say that Jesus is God's beloved Son, in Whom God is well pleased. Matthew, Mark, and Luke gave the same account. They all stated that the voice of God spoke and said that Jesus is His Beloved Son, in Whom He is well pleased.

If this truth is understood that Jesus' transfiguration prefigures His coming, as outlined above, then you are ready for the next layer of truth concerning the coming of our Lord Jesus Christ. Peter's account of the transfiguration is called Jesus' "coming." Thus, if one reads the gospel of Matthew, Mark, and Luke, the approximate "times and seasons" (plural) of Jesus' coming can also be extrapolated to be **after** six thousand years and to be **about** the eighth thousand years.

> ^{1}***And after six days** Jesus taketh Peter, James, and John his brother, and brings them up into a high mountain apart,* $^{17:2}$*And was transfigured before them ....* **(Matthew 17:1-2).**
>
> ***And after six days** Jesus taketh with him Peter, and James, and John, and leads them up into a high mountain apart by themselves: and he was **transfigured before them (Mark 9:2).***
>
> ***And it came to pass about ... eight days** after these sayings, he took Peter and John and James, and went up into a mountain to pray.* ^{29}*And as he prayed, the fashion of his countenance was altered ...* **(Luke 9:28).**

In the accounts above that prefigures Jesus' coming, all three gospels gave the time when the **transfiguration (Jesus' power and coming)** took place. Matthew and Mark said that it was *"after six days."* Luke said that it happened *"about eight days after* Jesus' sayings."

Thus, the event of Jesus' transfiguration literally happened after six days, or around eight days after Jesus made His declaration. Jesus stated that there were "some" (Peter, James, and John) standing with Him who would see Jesus' coming in His kingdom.[34] They did indeed see Jesus come in His kingdom before they died. They saw it after six (6) days to eight (8) days later.

The phrases *"after six days" "about eight days"* may prophetically point to thousands of years also. That is, six days can also equate to six thousand years. Eight days can also represent eight thousand years.

Peter declared:

> *"that **one day** is with the Lord as **a thousand years**, and a **thousand years** as **one day**" (2 Peter 3:8).*

Peter's principle of the thousand years-day principle provides some understanding into the plan of God concerning Jesus' coming. According to 2 Peter 1:16-18, the whole transfiguration experience prefigures Jesus' coming. Thus, the **approximate** times and seasons of Jesus' physical coming can also be understood relative to the three days (3,000 years) left in the prophetic week (7,000 years), after Jesus came (4,000 years from the first Adam), died, resurrected, and returned to heaven. According to Paul, the coming of the Lord will occur in the times and seasons of the night. However, Paul also said that day will not overtake us (surprise us) like a thief in the night. Only the

---

[34] Matthew 16:28

unsaved will be surprised by the coming of the Lord, not the sons of light, those in Christ.

> ¹⁵For this we say to you by the word of the Lord, that we who are alive and remain **until the coming of the Lord,** will not precede those who have fallen asleep. ¹⁶For the Lord Himself will descend from heaven with a shout, with the voice of the archangel and with the trumpet of God, and the dead in Christ will rise first. ¹⁷Then we who are alive and remain will be caught up together with them in the clouds to meet the Lord in the air, and so we shall always be with the Lord. ¹⁸Therefore, comfort one another with these words. ⁵:¹Now **as to the times and the epochs**, brethren, you have no need of anything to be written to you. ²For you yourselves know full well that the day of the Lord will come **just like a thief in the** night.... ⁴But you, brethren, are not in darkness, that the day would overtake you like a thief ... **(1 Thessalonians 4:15 - 5:5, NAU).**

With all that said, let us now discuss the concept of one day with the Lord is like a thousand years. First, let us establish that Jesus first came at the beginning of the fourth (4ᵗʰ) millennium after Adam's fall. We are now approximately six (6) millennia from Adam, or two (2) millennia from when Jesus came. We are about to begin, or have begun, the seventh (7ᵗʰ) millennium from the first Adam, or the third (3ʳᵈ) millennium from Jesus' death, burial, and resurrection and physical return to heaven.

> But do not forget this one thing, dear friends: With the Lord **a day is like a thousand years**, and a thousand years are like a day (2 Peter 3:8, NIV).

> And **after six days** Jesus ...was transfigured before them ... (Matthew 17:1-2)

> *And ... **about** ... **eight days** after these sayings ... as he prayed, the fashion of his countenance was altered ... (Luke 9:28-29)*

If the accounts of Peter, Matthew, Mark, and Luke are correct, and the Scripture cannot be broken, then Jesus can return physically "after six days," "about eight days." That is, **"after"** six thousand years from the first Adam, the Lord should return. The Scriptures show that Jesus <u>did not</u> transfigure (a type of His coming) on the sixth (day), He was transfigured **after** the sixth (6th) day.

Thus, all who were declaring that Jesus would come any minute, before the end of this sixth millennium from the first Adam, were incomplete in their teachings. How do we know that it is incomplete teaching to declare their predicted "rapture" will occur before the end of the six thousandth year from Adam and Eve?

First, Jesus did not come as they erroneously prophesied. Second, we are just at the close of the sixth (6th) day (6,000 years) from the first Adam, and Jesus was transfigured **"after"** the sixth (6th) day, **not before.** This can prophetically mean that the coming of our Lord Jesus Christ can happen **"after"** the six thousand years (6000) from the first Adam. Notice: I did not say his coming "will happen" at a certain time, I am saying that it "can (ability) happen."

Thus, Jesus' physical coming in His flesh and bone form (the same way He went to heaven) may <u>probably</u> be after this sixth millennium from the first Adam. We are approximately six days from the first Adam, or according to Peter's thousand years-day principle; we are approximately six thousand (6,000) years from the first Adam. We are at the close of the sixth millennium from the first Adam. That is, we are in the overlap between the sixth and seventh millennium. It also seems that there will be a coming of the Lord about the eighth day as this coming relates to God permanently inhabiting the temple of God (His Church) by His Spirit. Remember that Paul defined the exact coming of the Lord Jesus as "times" (plural) and "seasons" (plural).

Thus, as previously stated, if Matthew and Mark's accounts are correct—and they are—the Scriptures cannot be broken. And if Luke's account is correct—and it is—then this Scripture also cannot be voided. **What is a revelation of the two accounts— "after six days," "about eight days?"** If we follow Matthew and Mark's account Jesus can indeed come **"after"** six thousand years from the first Adam.

Therefore, there appears to be an overlap between the end of the sixth millennium and the beginning of the seventh millennium. I believe the time of the overlap is the transition between the sounding of the seventh or last trumpet and the beginning of the millennium reign of the saints with Christ.[35] With that said, let us look at some Scriptures that demonstrate that the Lord may come during the "seventh trumpet," which is the same trumpet as the "last trumpet," which is also called the "trumpet of God."

> *John to the seven churches which are in Asia: Grace be unto you, and peace, from him which is, and which was, and **which is to come. (Revelation 1:4).***

---

[35] There was a transition from Law to Grace of approximately 40 years, after Jesus' ascension, AD 70. Also, "man" is a variable of time, like Moses was a variable of time that delayed the deliverance of the sons of Israel from Egypt by 30 years (30 years beyond the original 400 years God designated in Genesis 15:13. See Genesis 15:13 with Exodus 12:41 and Galatians 3:17 and 2 Peter 3:12.

*John, to the seven churches which are in Asia: Grace be to you and peace from Him who is, and who was, and **who is to come*** **(Revelation 1:4, English Majority Text Version)**

*I am Alpha and Omega, the beginning, and the ending, says the Lord, which is, and which was, and **which is to come**, the Almighty* **(Revelation 1:8).**

*I am the Alpha and Omega," says the Lord God ... **He who is to come**, The Almighty* **(Revelation 1:8, English Majority Text Version).**

*And the four beasts ... rest not day and night, saying, Holy, holy, holy, Lord God Almighty, which was, and is, and **is to come*** *(Revelation 4:8).*

*And the living beings ... never rest day or night, saying, Holy, holy, holy, Lord God Almighty, He who was, and who is, and **is to who is to come*** *(Revelation 4:8, English Majority Text Version).*

*We give thee thanks, O Lord God Almighty, which art, and was, **and are to come**; because you have taken to thee thy great power ....* **(Revelation 11:17).**

*We give you thanks, O Lord God Almighty, **the One who is and who was**, because You have taken Your great power* **(Revelation 11:17, English Majority Text Version).**

*We give You thanks, O Lord God, the Almighty, **who are and who were**, because You have taken Your great power* **(Revelation 11:17, NAU).**

In the verses above with regards to the King James Version, we see the phrases that indicate that the Lord Almighty "was," "is" and **"is to come."** However, the King James Version is only translated from one (1) text, while the Majority Text is translated from over five thousand (5,000) texts. The New American Standard Bible (updated version) was translated from a few Alexandrian Texts. With that said, in Revelation 11:17, in all the manuscripts except for one, they all excluded the phrase "who is to come."

Again, with regards to the verses listed above, most of the Greek manuscripts say **"He is to come"** until we get to Revelation 11:17. In Revelation 11:17, "He is to come" is not mentioned anymore; and Revelation 11:17 is to occur during the seventh trumpet. Again, this seventh trumpet is also defined as the "last trumpet" or "the trump pf God" by the apostle Paul.

That is, when the seventh trumpet sounds, the phrase "He who is to come" is not in the oldest Greek texts. The oldest manuscripts excluded the phrase. Why did the Holy Spirit exclude that phrase after the seventh trumpet (the last of seven trumpets)? Because, "the coming of the Lord will be "in" the seventh trumpet which Paul also calls the "last trumpet." So, it appears to me that the phrase "He who is to come" is excluded from Revelation 11:17 because at the seventh (or last) trumpet is included in the times and seasons when the Lord Jesus comes.

In other words, there is no need to say "He is to come" if it is during the seventh trumpet the Lord comes. According to Paul, in the second book of Thessalonians, the Lord comes during the **"trumpet of God." At which time,** the dead in Christ first will be the first to rise. And according to, 1 Corinthians 15:51-52, the resurrection to inherit the kingdom of God occurs in the **last trumpet** where mortality will be swallowed up with immortality. It follows that the same is true for the seventh trumpet (the last trumpet of the seven trumpets).

*15For ... we who are alive and remain until the coming of the Lord will by no means precede those who are asleep. 16For the Lord Himself will descend from heaven ... **with the trumpet of God**. And the dead in Christ will rise first* **(1 Thessalonians 4:15-16: NKJ)**

51Behold, I tell you a mystery: We shall not all sleep, but we shall all be changed -- 52in a moment, in the twinkling of an eye, **at the last trumpet**. *For the* **trumpet will sound**, *and* **the dead will be raised incorruptible**, *and we shall be changed* **(1 Corinthians 15:51-52, NKJ)**.

15The **seventh angel sounded his trumpet** .... *16And the twenty-four elders ... worshiped God, 17saying: "We give thanks to you, Lord God Almighty, the One who is and who was, because you have taken your **great power** and have begun to reign* **(Revelation 11:15-17, NIV)**.

All three of the texts above agree in heralding the physical coming of the Lord. In His coming, the "trumpet of God" will sound, and the dead in Christ will rise first. The "last trumpet" will sound and the dead will be raised incorruptible. The seventh trumpet sounded, and no mention of the Lord's future coming occurs because He came during that trumpet, and resurrection also occurred because the Lord Almighty used His "great power" of resurrection as seen in Revelation 11:17 with Acts 4:33.

And the **seventh angel sounded his trumpet;** *and there were great voices in heaven, saying, "The kingdoms of this world has become the kingdoms of our Lord, and of His Christ; and He shall reign forever and ever.... We give you thanks, O Lord God Almighty,* **the One who is and who was,** *because You have taken Your **great power**, and have begun to reign* **(Revelation 11:15; 17, EMTV)**.

> *And with* **great power** *gave the apostles* **witness of the resurrection of the Lord Jesus: and** *great grace was upon them all* **(Acts 4:33).**

During the sounding of the seventh angel with his seventh trumpet, the Lord will be worshipped for taking His "great power," and He will also be worshipped for His reign. What is this "great power?" According to the book of Acts, God's "great power" is associated with Jesus' resurrection power. "With **great power** gave the apostles **witness of the resurrection of the Lord Jesus.**"

In 1 Thessalonians 4:13-18, we learn that a trumpet will sound, and there will be resurrection in Jesus' coming. In 1 Corinthians 15:52, we also learn that the trumpet mentioned in Thessalonians is the "last trumpet." In the book of Revelation, there are seven trumpets; therefore, the seventh trumpet of the seven trumpets in the book of Revelation is the last trumpet. In the seventh trumpet, God's "great power" is acknowledged in the worship of the living creatures and the twenty-four elders.

That is, it appears that during the seventh trumpet, the Lord comes, and resurrection occurs during His coming. He took "His great power" of resurrection and ruled. As a result, there is no need for the elders and the living creatures to say in their worship that Jesus is to come, because He must have returned during the seventh trumpet

With that said, lets us now look at the possible coming of the Lord **"about** eight days" (about 8,000 years from when Adam was created).

> *And ...* **about** *...* **eight days** *after these sayings ... as he prayed, the fashion of his countenance was altered ....* **(Luke 9:28-29).**

The Greek word translated "about" is the Greek word **"hosei"** which is defined as: **"as if"** according to Strong's Concordance. **"Hosei"** is a compound of two words "hos" (which how) and "ei" (if). Let us now insert the definition into the text and see how it reads. "And ... **'as if'** eight days ... the fashion of his countenance was altered." Or, **"'which if'** eight days ... the fashion of his countenance was altered." Or, **"'how if'** eight days ... the fashion of his countenance was altered."

Thus, when Jesus was transfigured, which Peter called Jesus' "power and **coming,**" this "coming" happened **"as if"** it was the eighth day. The power and coming happened **"how"** it would be **"if"** it was the eighth day. It was Jesus' power and coming on the holy mount **"which"** happened as it would be **"if"** it was the eighth day.

With that said, using Peter's thousand years-day principle, Jesus' transfiguration happened **"as if"** it was the eighth (8th) thousand year from Adam, according to God's time. His transfiguration happened **"how"** it will be **"if"** it was the eighth thousand year in God's time, the beginning of God's new week.

Since Solomon's temple is one of the patterns of the Church of Jesus, (the "permanent" temple that Jesus is building) then the Lord may not be finished building His temple until after the seventh (7th) year, just as Solomon took seven and a half (7 ½) years to build the temple. **Note**: That the Holy of Holies built by King Solomon (20 Cubits x 20 Cubits x 20 Cubits=8,000 Cubits³ which may point to 8,000 cubits of years).

> *37In the fourth year the foundation of the house of the LORD was laid, in the month of Ziv. 38And in the eleventh year, in the month of Bul, which is the eighth month, the house was*

*finished in all its details and according to all its plans. So, he was **seven years** in building it **(1 Kings 6:37-38, NKJ).***

Solomon started building the temple in the fourth (4th)[36] year of his reign, in the second month (Ziv). He completed it in the 11th year of his reign, in the eighth month (Bul). Eleven minus four, equals seven (11-4=7), plus six months after the month he started. Solomon started in the second month ("Ziv"); and he finished building in the eighth month ("Bul"). Thus, Jesus' temple may also not be completed until the seventh millennium; and as the Lord's glory filled Solomon's temple with a "cloud" **after** the temple was finished;[37] the same thing is to happen after the Lord finishes building His temple. His temple will be for **"a habitation of God through the Spirit."**

> *[19]Now, therefore, you are no longer strangers and foreigners, but fellow citizens with the saints and members of the household of God, [20]having been built on the foundation of the apostles and prophets, Jesus Christ Himself being the chief cornerstone, [21]in whom the whole building, being joined together, grows into a **holy temple in the Lord**, [22]in whom you also are being built together for a **dwelling place of God in the Spirit** (Ephesians 2:19-22, NKJ).*
>
> *[1]So all the work that Solomon had done for the house of the LORD **was finished** .... [3]Therefore all the men of Israel assembled with the king at the feast, which was in the **seventh month** .... that the house, **the house of the LORD, was filled with a cloud**, [14]so that the priests could not continue*

---

[36] Jesus also started building His Church (the Temple of God) the fourth (4th) millennium from Mr. and Mrs. Adam's fall.
[37] 2 Chronicles 5:13-14

*ministering because of the cloud; for the **glory of the LORD filled the house of God** (2 Chronicles 5:1; 3; 13-14, NKJ).*

We should also understand that as the boards of the tabernacle built by Moses continued into the Holy of Holies, Thus, the Church will also continue in the millennium. That is, the "boards" are symbolic of the Body of Christ. As the Holy Place is symbolic of the current era of Jesus' Church; the Holy of Holies is also symbolic of the millennium rule of Christ and His resurrected saints <u>with</u> Him. The "boards" of the tabernacle of Moses not only encompass the Church age (the Holy Place of 2,000 cubits); but they also made up the millennium age (the Holy of Holies of 1,000 cubits).

So, the Church will continue to be built and purged during the millennium after which God will inhabit His Church through the Spirit permanently. In other words, just because the first resurrection occurred, it does not mean that the Church will not continue during the millennium. One of the reasons is that Satan will be bound and his deception controlled; and all influence of the three beasts must be purged from humanity.

Believe it, or not, the number of the beast won't be fully purged from some in the earth for another thousand after the first resurrection. Even though the beast and the false prophet were cast into the lake of fire just before the beginning of the seventh millennium, their influence must be washed away with fire. God is still delivering man from the beastly nature, including delivering mankind from being subject to death, like beasts.[38] At the end of the seventh millennium, Satan, Death and Hell will be completely vanquished

---

[38] Ecclesiastes 3:19

Satan will have his day in the lake of fire! The Lord will judge him and others after the seventh day. This is when Jesus **comes** to sit on the throne of His glory.

> *[31]"When the Son of Man comes in His glory, and all the holy angels with Him, then He will sit on the throne of His glory. [32]"All the nations will be gathered before Him, and He will separate them ...[41]"Then He will also say to those on the left hand, 'Depart from Me ... into the **everlasting fire** prepared for the devil and his angels ...'"* **(Matthew 25:31-32; 41, NKJ).**

The reference above shows another way to ascertain that Jesus will also **come** <u>after</u> the seventh millennium. Notice, Jesus does say that "the Son of man [Jesus] will **come** in His glory and all the holy angels with Him." The same discourse given by Jesus also states that after this coming, Jesus will sit on the throne of His glory to issue eternal judgments.

It is <u>after</u> His coming in His glory to sit upon the throne of His glory that Jesus commands some to **"depart ... into the everlasting fire prepared for the devil and his angels." According to Revelation 20:10-15**, the devil and those who are not found written in the Book of Life are cast into the lake of fire and lightning <u>after</u> the millennium rule of Christ and the first resurrected saints who ruled with Christ is completed.

Thus, according to Matthew and John, it appears that Jesus will also come in glory after the seventh millennium at which time Gog and Magog is manifested; and at which time Satan and those not found written in the book of life will go to the lake of fire—the second death.

That is, just as people, angels and Satan were not sent to the lake of fire until after the millennium rule of the resurrected saints with Christ as described in Revelation 20:10-15, so likewise Matthew 25:31-46, indicates that the sending of some people and angels to the lake of fire happens **after** Jesus comes in His glory to sit upon His throne. This coming appears to be **after** the end of the 7th millennium from the first Adam, which is also called the millennium rule of the first resurrection saints with Christ. In Revelation 20:11, the great white throne is declared after the seventh millennium is completed.

In other words, the Lord will manifest in His coming at the beginning of the seventh millennium to cast the beast, the false prophet into the lake of fire; and He will also destroy the nations that follow the beast and the false prophet, feeding them to birds from mid-heaven, at which time the strong angel will also bind Satan; and more importantly, "the dead in Christ will rise first" in Jesus' physical coming (return); **however,** it appears that Jesus will yet come again at the beginning of the eighth millennium to send Satan to the lake of fire. He will also be sending those who are not found written in the Book of Life to the lake of fire; then Death and Hell will also go to the lake of fire.

The next item that must be discussed relative to the man-made doctrine of the rapture is **so called great tribulation** that is to occur after their proposed rapture occurs. This concept of "the great tribulation" occurring after the rapture is not true according to Scripture in Revelation 7:14.

> *And I said unto him, Sir, you know. And he said to me, these are they which **came out of great tribulation**, and have washed their robes, and made them white in the blood of the Lamb **(Revelation 7:14).***

Here is how the Revelation 7:14 reads according to the tense it is was originally written in: "And I said to him, **Lord,** you

perceived. And he said to me, these are they which **are-coming out of the great tribulation,** and have washed their robes, and made them white in the blood of the Lamb."

"Are coming" is present tense in all the Greek texts. This means that the great tribulation happened in the days when John saw the vision. In other words, the phrase "came out" is not written in the future tense; it was written in the present tense. That is, the group of people in Revelation 7:9 came out of the great tribulation that was occurring in the days of John, approximately 2,000 years ago. With that said, for those who are afraid of "the great tribulation," the safest way to understand "the great tribulation" is with the Scriptures.

According to the Scriptures "great tribulation" is also related to the severe famine, or hunger in the days of Joseph, according to Acts 7:11. "Now a famine and **great 'tribulation'** came over all the land of Egypt and Canaan, and our fathers found no sustenance." "The great tribulation" is related to the persecution of the Church by the Roman Caesar in the days of John, or the great tribulation of "hunger," "thirst," "sun," and "heat" that some also experienced according to Revelation 7:16 coupled with Revelation 7:14.

The destruction of Jerusalem by Titus is also called great tribulation in Matthew 24:21. The great tribulation of Matthew 24 is also a past reality that occurred in AD 70. There were basically three questions asked by the disciple in Matthew 24; and Jesus answered all of them, including the "great tribulation" of that generation.

> [1]*Then Jesus went out and departed from the temple, and His disciples came up to show Him the buildings of the temple.* [2]*And Jesus said to them, "Do you not see all these things?*

Assuredly, I say to you, not one stone shall be left here upon another, that shall not be thrown down." ³Now as He sat on the Mount of Olives, the disciples came to Him privately, saying, "Tell us, when will these things be? And what will be the sign of Your coming, and of the end of the age?" (Matthew 24:1-3)

Question #1: When shall these things be that the stones be thrown down?

*¹⁵"Therefore when you see the 'abomination of desolation,' spoken of by Daniel the prophet, standing in the holy place" (whoever reads, let him understand), ¹⁶"then let those who are in Judea flee to the mountains. ¹⁷Let him who is on the housetop not go down to take anything out of his house. ¹⁸And let him who is in the field not go back to get his clothes ¹⁹But woe to those who are pregnant and to those who are nursing babies in those days! ²⁰And pray that your flight may not be in winter or on the Sabbath. ²¹For then there will be **great tribulation**, such as has not been since the beginning of the world until this time, no, nor ever shall be. ²²And unless those days were shortened, no flesh would be saved; but for the elect's sake those days will be shortened …²⁹"Immediately after **the tribulation of those days** the sun will be darkened, and the moon will not give its light; the stars will fall from heaven, and the powers of the heavens will be shaken. **(Matthew 24:15-22; 29)***

Jesus gave the answer in Matthew 24:15-29; and according to Jesus that generation which lived in His days would not pass way until all the things he answered the disciples happen (Matthew 24:34). In Jesus response he also defined "great tribulation," as the time of "the abomination of desolation" in which the temple would be destroyed and the destruction of Jerusalem occurred. Thus, I am not sure why some are trying to change Jesus' prediction. Titus threw down every stone in Jerusalem in AD 70; there was "great tribulation then; and it happen in that generation, as Jesus said. At the time, Jesus said to His disciples: "'Amen,' I say to you, **this generation** shall not pass, until all these things be fulfilled" (Matthew 24:34).

Question #2: What is the sign of Your coming?

Jesus gave the answer in Matthew 24:29-41. The sign of His coming is the sing of the Son of Man **coming** on the clouds of heaven. "Coming" is written in the present tense in the Greek text. Therefore, Jesus was presently coming on clouds, then, when He spoke these words. That is, His coming on clouds was a present reality at the time He answered His disciples' questions. With that said, what are the Clouds? See Hebrews 12:1; Jude 12 (negative sense). What does the sun, moon and star mean? See Genesis 37:9-11. What generation is "this generation" that Jesus referred to? The generation that Jesus live. Who was taken and who was left in the days of Noah? The wicked was taken and Noah was left—Genesis 7:23. Yet, with that said, the setting of Lot's wife and Noah prefigures the transition from this age into the millennium age ("the age 'impending'").

Question #3: What is the sign of the end of the age?

Jesus answered this question in Matthew 24:4-14. The gospel must be preached in all the world before the end (AD 70) comes. The gospel was preached in all the world as certified by Paul (Colossians 1:5-6, Colossians 1:23, Romans 15:21, Acts 15:21). The phrase "end[39] of the age is used in various places in the Bible

---

[39] End is the Greek word "suntelos" (together-finish, together-completion, etc.)

and it has more of a meaning of "completion" of the age (Matthew 24:3, Matthew 13:39; 40; 49, Matthew 28:20, Hebrews 9:28). The age of the Law was ended and the age of Grace was initiated through Jesus, and Grace is still being imparted through Jesus' Church. It follows that this age will be completed; and "the Sabbath age" (the seventh one thousand years of God's prophetic week) will be preeminent. It is worthy to note that the phrase "in these last days" in Hebrews 1:2 literally reads, "the last of these days." The last of what days? The last days of the age of the Law at that time.

The Doctrine of Giving

2 Corinthians 8:7, last part: ... *[see] that you abound in this grace also.*

One of the most abused areas in Christianity is the doctrine of giving and receiving. No one should be coerced or forced to give. The amount that one gives should not be defined by second or third parties. The Spirit of the Lord Jesus in His people specify how much one should give. The doctrine of tithe under the New Covenant is not enforced by the curse of the Law. Tithing is realized by revelation and blessings under the Melchizedek order of priesthood. Jesus is our High Priest after the order of Melchizedek.

> *18Then Melchizedek king of Salem brought out bread and wine; he was the priest of God Most High. 19And he blessed him and said: "Blessed be Abram of God Most High, Possessor of heaven and earth; 20and blessed be God Most High, Who has delivered your enemies into your hand." And he gave him a tithe of all* **(Genesis 14:18-20).**

Abram had just defeated some enemies and rescued Lot, his nephew. After the battle, Melchizedek, the King of Salem introduced himself to Abram by blessing Abram and blessing the Highest God. Hebrews 7:1 reinforced that Melchizedek **"met"** Abraham. After Melchizedek blessed Abram, Abram of his own free will or, by revelation of the blessing bestowed upon him, decided to tithe to Melchizedek. People who do not give or tithe at all have not really **"met"** Jesus, their Melchizedek. That is, once Jesus **meets** us, or we **meet** Jesus we will willingly tithe to Jesus. Why? Jesus blesses those He **meets**.

Thus, Abram tithed because he was blessed, not because he was cursed, and not because the Law says so. The curse of the Law did not exist at the time of Abraham. The book of Hebrews 7:4 said that Abraham tithed because he considered Melchizedek **"great,"** and **"vast."** This revelation of the "greatness" of Melchizedek came after he blessed Abram. Jesus did the same when He walked the earth. Jesus blessed people; and Melchizedek is a type of Jesus Christ our Lord and King.

> *¹For this Melchizedek, king of Salem, priest of the Most High God, who **met** Abraham returning from the slaughter of the kings and **blessed him,** ²to whom also Abraham gave a tenth part of all, first being translated "king of righteousness," and then also king of Salem, meaning "king of peace," ³without father, without mother, without genealogy, having neither beginning of days nor end of life, but **made like the Son of God,** remains a priest continually. ⁴Now consider how **great** this man was, to whom even the patriarch Abraham gave a tenth of the spoils* **(Hebrews 7:1-4).**

Melchizedek is "**made like the Son of God.**" Thus, as Jesus bestowed the blessings of salvation upon us, we should tithe to Him. Saying it another way, when we tithe to Jesus, we declare that Jesus is "considered" "great," and "vast" towards us. We tithe because we believe that Jesus is great. We tithe because Jesus has "blessed us with all spiritual blessings in the heavenly" (Ephesians 1:3). **Tithing, according to the New Testament, is also us witnessing that Jesus is indeed resurrected.**

> *⁶but he [Melchizedek] whose genealogy is not derived from them received tithes from Abraham and **blessed** him who had the promises. ⁷Now beyond all contradiction the lesser is blessed by the better. ⁸Here mortal men receive tithes, but there he receives them, of whom it is **witnessed that he lives** (Hebrews 7:6-8).*

It is "witnessed" that the Melchizedek of Genesis 14 "lives." That is, Melchizedek never died; he did not have an "end of life;" He is "made like the Son of God, remains a priest continually." Thus, when we tithe, we are testifying that Jesus is indeed resurrected! Jesu lives! We are testifying that Jesus "continues" as the High Priest "into the age." We tithe because Jesus lives! We tithe because Jesus blessed us! We tithe because Jesus is "great." Jesus is our "Great High Priest." We are no longer under the curse of the law.

> *10For as many as are of the works of the law are under the curse; for it is written, "Cursed is everyone who does not continue in all things which are written in the book of the law, to do them." 11But that no one is justified by the law in the sight of God is evident, for "the just shall live by faith." 12Yet the law is not of faith, but "the man who does them shall live by them." 13**Christ has redeemed us from the curse of the law,** having become a curse for us (for it is written, "Cursed is everyone who hangs on a tree"), 14that the **blessing** of Abraham might come upon the Gentiles in Christ Jesus, that we might receive the promise of the Spirit through faith **(Galatians 3:10-14).***

Ministers cannot use the doctrine of "curses" to force people to tithe. "Curses" are done away in Christ. "Christ has redeemed us from the curse of the law, having become a curse for us (for it is written, "Cursed is everyone who hangs on a tree")." Ministers can no longer use Malachi 3 as a catalyst to curse the saints. **You cannot and should not curse Christ to get money;** and the Church is also considered as Christ

> *For as the body is one and has many members, but all the members of that one body, being many, are one body, **so also is Christ** (**1 Corinthians 12:12**).*

For as many of you as were **baptized into Christ have put on Christ** *(Galatians 3:27).*

Thus, a person must be careful with respect to cursing the Church over tithes, that person may be cursing the Christ. When Paul (formerly Saul) was persecuting the Church, Jesus confronted Paul concerning Paul's persistent persecution of the Church. As Jesus introduced Himself to Paul, Jesus did not say to Paul, why are you persecuting my Church. On the contrary, Jesus equated the Church to Himself. Jesus said, "Saul, Saul, why are you persecuting **Me**" (Acts 9:4)?

The doctrine of using the curse of the Law to enforce tithing is not to be used against Christ's Church. Any curse against God's Church is done away in Christ. A minister is to use the doctrine of Melchizedek's blessings. The Bible said that the Law (the curse) which was "after" the promise cannot void the promises.

> *"And this I say, that the law, which was four hundred and thirty years* **later, cannot annul** *the covenant that was confirmed before by God in Christ, that it should make the promise of no effect"* **(Galatians 3:17).**

The blessings in Christ supersede the curse of the Law. We tithe because Jesus blessed us. We do not tithe because we are afraid of a curse. We tithe because of the promises of God by the revelation of Jesus Christ; and we tithe to the "house of God" (Bethel) and those who are "priest-together" with Jesus Christ in the Melchizedek order. This principle or doctrine is seen in an encounter that Jacob had with God.

> [10]*Now Jacob went out from Beersheba and went toward Haran.* [11]*So he came to a certain place and stayed there all night, because the sun had set. And he took one of the stones of that place and put it at his head, and he lay down in that place to*

sleep. ¹²*Then he dreamed, and behold, a ladder was set up on the earth, and its top reached to heaven; and there the angels of God were ascending and descending on it. ¹³And behold, the LORD stood above it and said: "I am the LORD God of Abraham your father and the God of Isaac; the land on which you lie I will give to you and your descendants. ¹⁴"Also your descendants shall be as the dust of the earth; you shall spread abroad to the west and the east, to the north and the south; and in you and in your seed all the families of the earth shall be blessed. ¹⁵"Behold, I am with you and will keep you wherever you go, and will bring you back to this land; for I will not leave you until I have done what I have spoken to you." ¹⁶Then Jacob awoke from his sleep and said, "Surely the LORD is in this place, and I did not know it." ¹⁷And he was afraid and said, "How awesome is this place! This is none other than the **house of God,** and this is **the gate of heaven!"** ¹⁸Then Jacob rose early in the morning, and took the **stone** that he had put at his head, set it up as a **pillar,** and poured **oil** on top of it. ¹⁹And **he called the name of that place Bethel**; but the name of that city had been Luz previously. ²⁰Then Jacob made a vow, saying, "If God will be with me, and keep me in this way that I am going, and give me bread to eat and clothing to put on, ²¹"so that I come back to my father's house in peace, then the LORD shall be my God. ²²"And this stone which I have set as a pillar shall be God's house, and of all that You give me I will surely **give a tenth** to You"* **(Genesis 28:10-22).**

Jacob received instruction from God via a dream that he had. After he woke up from the dream, Jacob determined that the "place" where he received the instruction from God was "none other than the house of God, and he called the name of that place Bethel." Jacob also made a vow there, by his own volition, to tithe to God, saying, "Of all that You give me I will surely give a tenth to You."

Jacob made this "vow" to tithe before the Law was given some hundreds of years later. Thus, tithe is not a legalistic principle; but an action born out of blessings. God blessed Jacob concerning the promise He made to Abraham and to Abraham's seed. As a result of the confirmation of God's promise to Jacob, Jacob decided to give God the tithe. Jacob also indicated that the "place" where he would present the Lord with his tithe would be "God's house." Thus, the house of God, the Church of the living God is the place where we also tithe. The book of Hebrew also teaches that the "priests-together" with Christ in the Melchizedek order should also receive tithe from the people of God.

With that said, here is the big question, do we tithe from our gross pay, or do we tithe from our net pay? **The answer is yes!** Both statements are true. If we tithe from the gross, then if we earn a tax return, then you do not have to tithe from the tax return. If you tithe from a net income, then you should tithe from your tax return. Abraham tithed from a tenth of all the spoil that was present with him after the battle. Paul said that we give according to what we "have."

"For if there is first a willing mind, it is accepted **according to what one has,** and **not according to what he does not have**" (2 Corinthians 8:12). Even Moses when he was directed by God to receive the offering to build the tabernacle, it was only for those who had "a willing heart;" and here is also an important point: Moses only told them **"what"** to give, he did not tell them **"how much"** to give.

This brings me to another point; I would like to discuss the doctrine of men presetting "how much" a person should give in meetings. The doctrine of $10,000 lines, $1,000 lines, $500 lines, $100 lines, $50 lines, and so on is not necessarily from God. It appears to be the greed and insecurities of man. With respect to the New Testament, the amount one gives is determined by the giver and/or the Holy Spirit. The amount one gives is not determined by the person receiving the gift.

Paul declared that the proper way to give is for each person to give themselves to God with respect to "how much" is to be shared. After, the Spirit of the Lord directs the individual giver, that person then gives accordingly. Here is Paul's statement: **"And not only as we had hoped, but they first gave themselves to the Lord,** and **then to us by the will of God"** (1 Corinthians 8:5). This truth is also borne out in Acts 5.

A husband and wife were removed from the earth (died) for lying to the Holy Spirit concerning their giving with respect to the amount they sold their land for. Their lie prompted Peter to ask them, "Didn't it belong to you before it was sold? And after it was sold, **wasn't the money at your disposal?** What made you think of doing such a thing? You have not lied to men but to God" (Acts 5:4). Peter made it clear that the amount one gives is at the **"disposal" (lit., authority)** of the giver. The Lord will indeed reveal His will to each believer as to how much to give; yet ultimately, the amount one gives is still in the authority of the giver.

Finally, there is prevalent practice of believer walking up to the pulpit area and throwing money at the speakers' feet. They use Acts 4:35 as their basis for this doctrine. This practice amounts to no more than the act of giving money to strippers. The practices of Acts 4:35 have a context.

In Acts 2 we learned that people came from all over the world to the Feast of Pentecost. After Peter and the eleven were filled with the Holy Spirit, Peter preached to the multitude that came to the feast; and "three thousand souls" were saved by believing in the Lord Jesus with their hearts. With that said, Acts 3 and Acts 4 are continuations of the thousands of souls that "were added" to the Lord in Acts 2. That is, it appears that the money was collected both for the "lacking" saints who lived at Jerusalem, and also for the thousands who traveled to Jerusalem from out of town to the Feast of Pentecost and remained there (for a time) after they were added to the Church by faith in Jesus Christ.

The visitors who received Christ in their lives may have run out of money if they stayed back for a time, and they may have needed help in addition to the saints who lived at Jerusalem that had "need." It is also important to note that the money that was laid at the apostles' feet was "**distributed to each** as anyone has need." The money was not collected into the pockets of the apostles solely for their so called "revelatory words." If it was so called revelation knowledge that caused people to give, Paul would have been an extremely rich man (compare 1 Corinthians 4:9-13); yet I am not saying that Paul did not eventually become comfortable financially (Acts 28:30-31, Philippians 4:12).

With that said, I am aware that Paul laid out the criteria for supporting widows. I am also aware that Paul said that if a man does not work, neither should he eat. However, if there is a "need," and if the Church has the funds, the need should be met without criticism. Listen to the heart of Apostle Paul:

> [32]"*So now, brethren, I commend you to God and to the word of His grace, which is able to build you up and give you an inheritance among all those who are sanctified.* [33]"*I have coveted no one's silver or gold or apparel.* [34]"*Yes, you yourselves know that* **these hands have provided for my necessities, and for those who were with me.*** [35]"*I have shown you in every way, by* **laboring** *like this, that you* **must**

support the weak. *And remember the words of the Lord Jesus, that He said,* **'It is more blessed to give than to receive'"** **(Acts 20:32-35).**

Reviewing Doctrines

In conclusion of this volume, we have seen that conferences were originally held to discuss doctrinal disputes in the Church. Yet, conferences for the saints at large should be held as general assemblies. "Israel after the flesh" had three major feasts per annum (the Feast of Passover, the Feast of Pentecost, and the Feast of Tabernacles). It appears to me that the Church can also have major spiritual feasts each year to worship "the Great-Togetherness," our heavenly Father, our King, Jesus and to hear from the Holy Spirit.

We also discussed the "wind of doctrine" that causes immature saints to vacillate in instability and be carried about through the gambling or competition of men. That is, doctrines invented by men cause instability in the immature. Ministers are to ensure that teachings are not a guessing game, but that teachers of Jesus allow themselves to be taught by the Holy Spirit, and by those whom God, the Father have called to give sound doctrines

It follows that we are to choose God's choice, God's will, God's pleasure, God's desire, God's inclination for our lives for us to know God's doctrine. As indicated, our Lord Jesus, Himself, said that we must "choose [God's] choice" so that we may "know the doctrine" that is "from" God as opposed to "the commands and doctrine of men." The Father's will is for us to become His "placed" "sons and daughters." The Father's will is that we know how to "possess our vessels (bodies) unto honor." In everything we are to give thanks to God; this is also God's desire.

Jesus' doctrine of His vision for His Church is part of the Father's will. One of the first orders of Jesus' vision is to mend the lives of all new saints. They are to be mended and fitted by Him to take their place in the Body of Christ. That is, after saints are mended by the five Christ-gifts, the saints are to do the work of the ministry, the work of service as prescribed by the Spirit of Jesus and His "priest-workers." In addition, Jesus' vision also includes the saints maturing to the point of edifying each other in love by "being true."

Next, we also discussed the doctrine of purpose. We learned that the Biblical definition of God's purpose for us is to become mature sons (male and female) in the earth. God's predetermined purpose for us is to be conformed to the image of the Son — Jesus. As the writer of Hebrews says, God wants to be "into us a Father," and we "into him a son." Yes, the purpose of our Father — the God of Jesus — is to have many "mature sons" whom He can "place" in His predetermined "glory" for them.

We also discussed the doctrine of duality, a common theme in this age is that unlearned ministers emphasize God and the Devil simultaneously. The is a serpent God created. The serpent is not in a class with God or God's sons. Just because the Satan "places" himself among God's sons, does not make a son or equal with God. In fact, Jesus judged the Devil; Jesus bound Satan. Jesus — the Stronger One, stripped Satan of the amour, his strength of deception. Jesus cast Satan out and judged him. Satan is now weaker — he is not strong enough to stand against Jesus, Michael, the arch angel, the Church of Jesus, and so on. We should preach the all-powerful God and marginalize the Devil.

The doctrine of self-appointment is also of import to recognize and abstain from those who are self-appointed. We should never self-appoint to any office God did not call us to. There was a king (Uzziah) who was not satisfied with being a king. He appointed himself a priest and attempted to offer incense on the Altar of

Incense. The king was smitten in the forehead with leprosy[40] for his presumption (2 Chronicles 26:16-20). This same principle is true for some today who have appointed themselves. Their minds are radiating the mark of the beast, rather than expressing the character of God.

The doctrine of rapture is a doctrine that most will not question, due to its popularity. In addition, there is no word "rapture" in the scripture. Some claim that the rapture will occur before the great tribulation. Some claim the rapture will occur during the middle of the great tribulation. Some also claim that the rapture will occur after the great tribulation. The book of Revelation teaches that the great tribulation started 2,000 years ago. We are still here even though the great tribulation was a "present" reality in the days of John, the apostle whom Jesus loved. The ministers of the Church of our Lord Jesus Christ need to examine their doctrines again. The ministers of the gospel need a revelation telling them to confer with other apostles who may have a revelation that was not previously published (compare Colossians 1:26).

Finally, the doctrine of giving really needs to be examined. The structure of giving in most Churches is just plain wrong. Giving is supposed to be voluntary, not forced by a second or third party. Moses told the people of Israel what to give, but not how much to give. Yes, we may define that people can give food, money, jewelry, houses, land, machinery, and so on. However, it does not appear that ministers should define lines by the amount a person gives and then issue prophecy accordingly. On the contrary, let us follow the pattern of giving as outlined by

---

[40] Leprosy is a symbol of being marked to isolation. In the case of Uzziah being smitten on the forehead with leprosy, his leprosy on the forehead is a symbol of the mark of the beast on the forehead.

the apostles Paul, Barnabas, Peter, etc. In conclusion of this book, I would like to leave you with Jesus' encouragement of how to know doctrine. We must allow God, the Holy Spirit to teach us.

> "Now about the middle of the feast Jesus went up into the temple and taught. ¹⁵And the Jews marveled, saying, 'How does this Man know letters, having never studied?' ¹⁶Jesus answered them and said, 'My doctrine is not Mine, but His who sent Me. **¹⁷If anyone wants to do His will, he shall know concerning the doctrine, whether it is from God** or whether I speak on My own authority. ¹⁸He who speaks from himself seeks his own glory; but He who seeks the glory of the One who sent Him is true, and no unrighteousness is in Him'" **(John 7:14-18).**

Other Books

Poiema, by Judith Peart

Wisdom from Above, by Judith Peart

Sexual Healing, by Judith Peart

100 Nevers, by Judith Peart

The Shattered and the Healing by Judith Peart

The Lamb, by Donald Peart

Jesus' Resurrection, Our Inheritance, by Donald Peart.

Sex Pleasures, By Donald Peart

Forgiven 490, by Donald Peart w/Judith Peart!

The Days of the Seventh Angel, By Donald Peart

The Torah (The Principle) of Giving, by Donald Peart

The Time Came, by Donald Peart

The Last Hour, the First Hour, the Forty-Second Generation, by Donald Peart

Vision Real, by Donald Peart

The False Prophet, Alias, Another Beast V1, by Donald Peart

"the beast," by Donald Peart

Son of Man Prophesy Against the false prophet, by Donald Peart

The Many False Prophets (The Dragon's Tail), by Donald Peart

The Work of Lawlessness Revealed, by Donald Peart

When the Lord Made the Tempter, by Donald Peart

Examining Doctrine, Volume 1, by Donald Peart

Exousia, Your God Given Authority, by Donald Peart

The Numbers of God, by Donald Peart

The Completions of the Ages ... by Donald Peart

The Revelation of Jesus Christ, by Donald Peart

Jude—Translation and Commentary, by Donald Peart

Obtaining the Better Resurrection, by Donald Peart

Manifestations from Our Lord Jesus ...by Donald and Judith Peart).

Obtaining the Better Resurrection, by Donald Peart

The New Testament, Dr. Donald Peart Exegesis: *Jesus was the first to properly "exegesis" the heavenly Father. Exegesis means critical explanation or interpretation of a text, especially of Scriptures. However, "exegesis" is the Greek compound "ek," which means "out-of," that is something having its origin within that something; and "hegeomai," which means, to lead. That is, this publication contains a "reading-out" of some of the Greek compounds used in the original texts. For example, the Greek word translated "gospel" is the Greek compound "euaggelion" ("eu" (good, well) and "aggello" (to bring a message). Thus, an exegesis of this word is "good-message."*

The Tree of Life, By Dr. Donald Peart

The Spirit and Power of John, the Baptist by Dr. Donald Peart

The Shattered and the Healing by Judith Peart

Is She Married to a Husband? by Donald Peart

The Ugliest Man God Made by Donald Peart

Does Answering the Call of God Impact Your Children? by Donald Peart

Victory Out-of-the Beast-the Harvest of the Earth by Donald Peart

Contact Information:
Crown of Glory Ministries
P.O. Box 1041 Randallstown, MD 21133
crownofglorymaryland@gmail.com
Phone: 410-905-0308

www.ingramcontent.com/pod-product-compliance
Lightning Source LLC
Chambersburg PA
CBHW060410050426
42449CB00009B/1943